A
SHORT
HISTORY OF
GLASS

A
SHORT
HISTORY OF
GLASS

by Chloe Zerwick

Harry N. Abrams, Inc., Publishers, New York
in association with
The Corning Museum of Glass

Redesigned and Updated Second Edition
Project Director: Robert Morton
Editor: Ruth A. Peltason
Designer: Dana Sloan

Corning Museum of Glass Photographers:
Raymond F. Errett and Nicholas L. Williams

Editorial Note: All dimensions are given in centimeters. One inch
equals 2.54 centimeters.

Page 2:
Enameled and gilded vase
Damascus, c. 1320–1330.
Height 30.2 cm

Pages 6–7:
Aquatint after J.M. Volz by C. Meichelt (From Glashütte im "Aule"
[Early Nineteenth Century Glassmaking in the Black Forest] by
A. Schreiber. Freiburg, 1820–1827.)

Page 9: *The Corning Museum of Glass*

Library of Congress Cataloging-in-Publication Data

Zerwick, Chloe.
  A short history of glass / by Chloe Zerwick.
    p. cm.
  Includes bibliographical references.
  ISBN 0-8109-3801-4. — ISBN 0-87290-121-1 (pbk. : Corning
Museum)
  1. Glass—History. I. Corning Museum of Glass. II. Title.
TP849.Z47 1990
666'.1'09—dc20   89-17779
                                      CIP

Glass is more gentle, graceful, and noble than any metal and its use is more delightful, polite, and sightly than any other material at this day known to the world.

Antonio Neri, 1612

CONTENTS

FOREWORD

People have been making glass for at least thirty-five
centuries. About 1,500 years before the birth of Jesus, back when
iron was first used, back when Moses led the Israelites out of
Egypt, glass was new. That was a very long time ago—in fact,
175 successive generations have gone by. Since those ancient
days, uncounted thousands of people in almost every part of the
world—people with traditions, needs, and ideas as varied as
history itself—have worked with glass. To discover and bring all
this human activity together is the task of The Corning Museum
of Glass: we do it by collecting and analyzing evidence. The best
source is the glass object itself, because each piece is like a time
capsule reflecting the ideas of its maker and the techniques,
practices, and styles when it was made. So far, we have acquired
by gift and purchase more than 24,000 glass objects. Archeology
gives us more evidence, recording as it does the lives of people,
of communities, of civilizations in which glass has played a part.
But the source that multiplies the fastest is the printed word. The
Museum's Rakow Library, which houses the world's most
comprehensive collection of publications on glass, contains more
than 50,000 items.

The Museum building, designed by architect Gunnar
Birkerts, opened in 1980. Textured glass panels, vacuum-
sputtered with stainless steel on the back, sheathe the upper floor
of the building and create a subtle mirrored effect while
reflecting solar heat. The unusual periscopic mirror system along
the outside wall enables visitors to see outside. This way both the
outside and daylight—but little damaging sunlight—are brought
indoors.

This concise history is a summary—shown mainly in
pictures—of the experiences, technical discoveries, and limitless

artistic inventions of the past 3,500 years. Wherever possible, passages from letters and important documents of the day are quoted. These, like the pieces themselves, are direct evidence, and give a lively idea of just what people thought about glass throughout history.

Dwight P. Lanmon
Director
The Corning Museum of Glass

INTRODUCTION

Glass: shiny, hard, fragile—shattering in an instant or surviving for thousands of years; a rigid liquid worked in a molten state—too hot to touch, yet often made by hand; molded, blown, cut, engraved, enameled, or painted. Of the craftsman, it demands the ultimate in steady nerves, skill, control, patience, judgment, and spontaneity. To possess such rigorous qualifications requires not only native gifts but also long experience, so it is no wonder that the head glassmaker is called a "gaffer," a word of respect used for an older person, dating back to the sixteenth century. The gaffer's reheating furnace is called a "glory hole," a tribute to the beauty he creates in the fire.

Though some glass objects have been as precious as gold, glass can be formed by melting together the most ordinary natural materials, found nearly everywhere: sand, the main ingredient of glass; ashes (alkali), usually made by burning certain plants or trees, to cause the sand to melt at a feasible temperature; and a stabilizing substance such as lime, made from crushed stones, to protect the glass against moisture. Virtually

(From Diderot and others, Encyclopédie. *18th century)*

the same glass recipe as that given on a cuneiform tablet of the seventh century B.C. is in use today.

The invention of glass more than 3,500 years ago is shrouded in uncertainty. The Roman historian Pliny attributed it to Phoenician sailors. He recounted how they landed on a beach, propped a cooking pot on some blocks of natron (an alkali) they were carrying as cargo, and made a fire over which to cook a meal. To their surprise, the sand beneath the fire melted and ran in a liquid stream that then cooled and hardened into glass. Today, scholars believe that glass evolved from the manufacture of faience, an older material with a white interior and a colorful, shiny surface. Faience, which can be made at a lower temperature than glass, is composed of crushed quartz and alkali. These same ingredients, mixed in slightly different proportions, form a true glass if subjected to a higher temperature.

That said, however, no one really knows how glass came to be made. It is older than the Ten Commandments and probably originated somewhere in the Middle East. It was adopted by the Romans, who contributed significantly to its development; it flowered under the Islamic empire; and it reached new heights in Renaissance Venice, whence it spread throughout Europe and eventually to America. In ancient Egypt, glass was a rare luxury;

today, it touches nearly every facet of our day. We drink our breakfast juice from it, cook in it, make lighting devices of it, keep out the weather with it, and use it in television sets, automobiles, medical equipment, communication devices, and spaceships. It is difficult to imagine life without it. With glass now in the hands of artists as well as craftsmen, with wires of glass threads transmitting light impulses across the land, with eyeglasses that lighten and darken with the sun, we may be seeing—within all the wonders of this long history—only the beginning.

Glass has also had its curious uses. Perhaps because it glittered with captured light, the ancients regarded it with awe and used it in magical amulets. The Chinese of early times customarily put glass cicadas, imitating those made of jade, on the tongues of the dead because the cicada was a symbol of life renewed after death. Napoleon lies under a shroud woven of glass fibers. Crystal balls, usually made of glass, are traditional foretellers of the future: steady gazing into their reflective depths may induce hallucinations that seem like distant events (crystallomancy is the name of this type of fortune-telling). In the eighteenth century, hollow glass spheres called "witch balls" were hung in English cottages to ward off evil spirits.

Whole orchestras have played glass instruments. Wigs with hair of spun glass have been made, and a spun glass dress was fashioned for Princess Eulalia of Spain in 1893. Victorian ladies carried glass hand coolers in the shape of eggs to cool their warm palms while dancing or being wooed.

Glass is an important part of many legends. Among the most persistent is that which relates how Alexander the Great, the third-century B.C. conqueror, descended into the sea in a huge glass jar to observe the plants and fishes there. Many Persian and Renaissance illustrations depict him in royal finery beneath the waves in his transparent bell, suspended by two ropes held by courtiers in a tiny boat on the water's surface.

In myths and fairy tales and also in Scripture, glass is often a symbol of clarity, spiritual perfection, and revelation. Being solid yet transparent, it is used as a metaphor for a level of existence between the visible and the invisible, or between the mundane and the mysterious. Messengers from the Celtic otherworld, for example, sometimes arrive by sea in glass boats, symbolizing the spiritual character of their mission. In Revelation 4:6, it is told that before the very throne of heaven "there was a sea of glass like unto crystal."

Glass mountains are often features of folk tales, to be climbed by the hero before he can win the princess, and the perfect fit of a glass slipper is the test of a true princess. The folk hero often comes upon a glass palace after leaving the dark forest, as though coming upon the clarity of truth after the ordeal of ignorance. In the Celtic realm of the gods, a lofty glass castle manned by ghostly sentinels is the abode of the Perfect One. King Arthur's soul is housed in a glass castle in Avalon. Irish and Welsh legends tell of glass castles that are island shrines surrounded by glassy water.

These myths, marvels, and curiosities indicate the powerful fascination that glass has held for the human imagination. Samuel Johnson, writing on the subject in the *Rambler,* an eighteenth-century publication, noted:

Who, when he first saw the sand or ashes . . . melted into a metallic form . . . would have imagined that, in this shapeless lump, lay concealed so many conveniences of life? . . . Yet, by some such fortuitous liquefaction was mankind taught to procure a body . . . which might admit the light of the sun, and exclude the violence of the wind; which might extend the sight of the philosopher to new ranges of existence, and charm him, at one time, with the unbounded extent of material creation, and at another, with the endless subordination of animal life; and, what is of yet more importance, might . . . succour old age with subsidiary sight. Thus was the first artificer in Glass employed, though without his knowledge or expectation. He was facilitating and prolonging the enjoyment of light, enlarging the avenues of science, and conferring the highest and most lasting pleasures; he was enabling the student to contemplate nature, and the beauty to behold herself.

GLASS IN PRE-ROMAN TIMES

A natural glass, obsidian, was formed millions of years ago by volcanic activity. The intense heat fused masses of silica in a translucent brown-black glass, and from this hard material early man chipped tools and weapons.

Little is known about man's first efforts to make glass. It is believed that glassmaking was discovered, perhaps accidentally, in Mesopotamia (now known as Iraq). Solid glass beads and amulets that may have been made as long ago as 2500 B.C. have been found. The pendant shown here (pl. 1) was made 1,000 years later. Later still, at the time of Tutankhamun (about 1350 B.C.), jewelry that combined glass with gold and colored stones was made for Egyptian royalty. The earliest hollow glass vessels (cups, bowls, bottles, etc.), which were more difficult to make than solid objects such as beads, appeared in Mesopotamia and Egypt in the sixteenth and fifteenth centuries B.C. By this date, the pyramids were already ancient monuments, although it was two centuries before Moses would receive the Ten Commandments. Thutmose III (1490–1437 B.C.) established an Egyptian empire in the Middle East and traded with Phoenicia, Crete, and the Aegean Islands. It is possibly after Thutmose had pushed into Mesopotamia and brought back glass that Egyptians learned how to make it.

Though the Egyptians were sophisticated enough to have had an irrigation system, a canal connecting the Nile to the Red Sea, writing, a knowledge of geometry, and contraceptives, the Egyptian glassmaker often used methods that seem primitive to us. To create glass containers (pl. 3), for example, he first made a core of clay combined with dung. He then wound hot glass around the core. The glass was reheated and smoothed by rolling

3.
Core-formed handled jar
Egypt, 1400–1360 B.C.
Height 11.8 cm
(50.1.1)

1.
Star pendant
Northern Mesopotamia, 1450–1350 B.C. Diameter 4.5 cm
(63.1.26)

it on a flat surface. Next, the glassmaker trailed glass threads of brilliant colors—turquoise, blue, yellow, red, white—around the surface and dragged them up and down to form waves or feathery patterns. When the vessel was finished, he picked out the clay core with a pointed instrument. This technique is known as core-forming.

In Egypt, no one but pharaohs, high priests, and nobles owned glass. Along with gold, silver, lapis lazuli, turquoise, ivory, alabaster, and carnelian, it enriched their thrones, funeral masks, mummy cases, and magical protective jewelry. On the dressing tables of wealthy women stood glass containers of rare ointments, scents, cosmetics, and oils. The wig-wearing, pleasure-loving aristocrats of ancient Egypt placed a high value on glass vases, jugs, bowls, cups for beer, and even miniature sculpture (pl. 2).

Elsewhere during this period (around the middle of the second millennium B.C.), Stonehenge was being built in Britain, the Chinese had learned to weave silk and to domesticate fowl and water buffalo, and bathrooms were installed in the Minoan palaces on Crete.

At roughly the same time, an independent glass industry had developed in Mesopotamia, where vessels were core-formed in much the same manner as those made in Egypt.

2.

Head of Amenhotep II
1436–1411 B.C. Height 4 cm Though many ancient glass vessels have been found, ancient glass sculpture is extremely rare. This head of Amenhotep II, who preceded Tutankhamun by about sixty years as ruler of Egypt, is the earliest glass portrait known. Cast in blue glass, this sculpture turned a tan color during its long burial. (79.1.4)

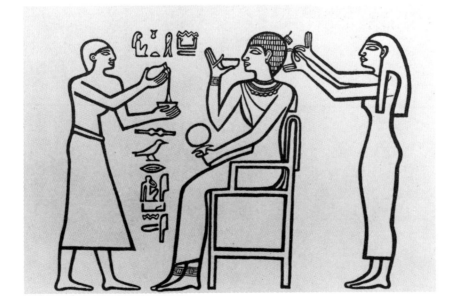

An Egyptian princess at her toilet. (From The Egyptians *by S. R. K. Glanville, London: A & C Black Ltd.)*

4.
Core-formed perfume bottle
Mesopotamia, 800–700 B.C.
Height 16.8 cm
(59.1.65)

Glassmaking declined between the thirteenth and ninth centuries B.C., though it may not have died out altogether. The industry was revived in Egypt, Mesopotamia, and elsewhere in the ninth century around the time of King David and King Solomon. (It has been said that when the Queen of Sheba visited King Solomon, she saw in the courtyard of his palace what she believed to be a pool of water. Accordingly, she tucked up her skirts so as not to wet them when she crossed, thereby revealing her regal limbs. Solomon then enlightened her by saying, "This is the palace evenly floored with glass.")

Core-forming persisted as an important glassmaking technique for many centuries, as demonstrated by the handled jars and perfume bottle on pages 15, 18, and 19, center. Some vessels were carved as if they were made of semiprecious stone. Other containers were cast in molds. After casting, the surface was ground and polished by wheels fed with abrasives. The result was known as cast glass.

Core-formed glass was usually opaque. However, Mesopotamian cast glass was often a transparent pale green (pl. 6). Many cast-glass shapes were similar to forms used in metal. The cast bowl illustrated (pl. 7) has a raised, hollow area in the middle—an omphalos—to permit a secure grip: the holder would put one finger inside the omphalos and his thumb firmly on the rim. Vessels of this type were probably made by filling molds with finely powdered glass and heating them until the powder melted. After cooling, the object was finished by grinding and polishing.

Egyptian glassmakers also made glass mosaics (pl. 9) from multicolored glass rods. The rods were bundled together to form a design, visible in cross sections. The bundle was fused, and the resulting large rod was heated and pulled out like taffy. The design remained the same, except that it got smaller and smaller as the rod became longer and longer. The rod was then cut into slices, each having the same identical design, which could be arranged in various patterns or used individually as decorative inlays.

6.

Cast and cut vase of greenish glass with lug handles

Mesopotamia or Syria, 725– 600 B.C. Height 19.2 cm The surface has been ground, probably by means of cutting wheels and abrasives.

(55.1.66)

5.

Core-formed handled jar

Eastern Mediterranean, 2nd– 1st century B.C. Height 24 cm Although it was made in the same manner as earlier core- formed objects, this jar was produced many centuries later.

(55.1.62)

7.

Cast and cut bowl

Probably Iran or Mesopotamia,
5th–4th century B.C.
Diameter 17.5 cm
In Aristophanes's play The
Archarnians *(425 B.C.),*
which was an attack on the
Peloponnesian War, the Greek
ambassador to the Persian
court relayed how "being guests
we perforce drank the undiluted
sweet wine from clear glass
vessels and gold plate."
Perhaps they drank from bowls
such as this nearly colorless
cast and cut glass bowl.
(59.1.578)

8.

Hellenistic cut bowl

Eastern Mediterranean, 3rd–
2nd century B.C. Height 6.4
cm, diameter 17 cm
(62.1.21)

9.

Mosaic glass plaque

Egypt, 1st century B.C. or A.D. Height 2.5 cm

Apis, the sacred bull, was worshiped as a form of the supreme Egyptian deity Osiris. Those who inhaled the bull's breath were thought to gain the gift of prophecy. The sacred bull was said to be the offspring of a virgin impregnated by a moonbeam. The Greek historian Herodotus reported that "Apis was a young black bull . . . on its forehead a white triangular spot." This spot can be seen on the plaque, which was probably inlaid on a piece of furniture. (59.1.97)

GLASS OF THE ROMAN EMPIRE

B y the time of the birth of Jesus, glassmaking was nearly half as old as it is now, but the most significant event in this long history—the discovery of glassblowing—had only just taken place. It probably occurred about 50 B.C. somewhere along the Syrian-Palestinian coast, then part of the Roman Empire.

The discovery of glassblowing was a major turning point in glass history. By blowing short puffs of air through a tube into a molten blob or "gather" of glass, rather than by casting or coreforming it, a glassmaker could quickly inflate a bubble of glass and work it into a great variety of sizes and shapes (pl. 10)—or he might expand the bubble in a mold, giving it both form and decoration in a single operation. The Roman discovery of glassblowing paved the way for the eventual mass production of glass.

From this moment on—by the use of sand, ashes, lime, fire, and his own breath—the glassmaker was able to produce an enormous and varied inventory. Glass was no longer exclusively a luxury product. In fact, it became more widely used for ordinary domestic purposes during the Roman Empire than at any subsequent time or place until the nineteenth century.

The Roman Empire at its height included what is now France, Spain, Portugal, England, Belgium, Switzerland, Turkey, the Middle East, Egypt, North Africa, and parts of the Netherlands, Germany, eastern Europe, and Austria. Therefore, what is called Roman glass could have come from any of these places during the first to fifth centuries A.D.

The popularity of Roman glass rested not only on its usefulness and reasonable price but also on its transparency and

Earliest known representation of glassblowing, found on a first-century A.D. Roman lamp. (Photograph courtesy Split Archeological Museum, Yugoslavia)

13.

Mold-blown ewer

Roman Empire, eastern Mediterranean or Italy, 1st century A.D. Height 23.8 cm The inscription "Ennion made me" is under the handle of the ewer. Ennion was probably a Syrian glassmaker who migrated to Italy. His glasses are considered to be the most elegant of all the Roman mold-blown ware. (59.1.76)

the beauty of its forms and colors. And, as Seneca (the Roman playwright and philosopher, and Nero's tutor) reasoned, the very fragility of the material further enhanced its popularity since "the desire to possess things increases with the danger of losing them."

According to the first-century historian Suetonius, a Roman glassmaker perfected unbreakable glass and presented a vase made of the material to the emperor Tiberius. The craftsman displayed the beautiful transparent vase to the emperor and then dashed it to the floor. It dented but did not break, and the workman easily repaired the dent with his hammer as though the vase were metal. Tiberius asked if the craftsman had told the secret of unbreakable glass to anyone. The workman proudly assured him that he had not, whereupon Tiberius had him put to death, fearing the glassmaker's secret would destroy the value of all the emperor's gold and silver. (Though some glass today is shatterproof, it cannot be worked with a hammer, and there is little doubt that the story is apocryphal.)

The Roman poet Horace said that despite glass's fragility, he much preferred a transparent drinking glass to a metal cup. "Let my eyes taste, too," he wrote.

Drinking cups of all shapes and sizes were available both for household use and for the lively public bars and eating places that were found in most Roman towns. The cups were used primarily for drinking wine, usually mixed with water, during and after the main meal of the day. Cups were also blown in molds, and some of them bore salutations such as "Rejoice and be merry," toasts that are still proclaimed 2,000 years later whenever a glass is raised.

Mold-blown bottles came in fanciful shapes: animals, grotesque human heads, grape clusters. Mold-blown souvenir beakers might be embellished with scenes of chariot races. Others bore scenes of bloody gladiatorial contests (pl. 11) in which men fought against each other or against wild beasts; thousands of animals might be slaughtered in one day, to the

10.
Roman glass vessels
Roman Empire, 1st–4th century A.D. Height (tallest) 28.3 cm
The invention of glassblowing made possible an enormous variety of vessels.

11.
Gladiator beaker
Roman Empire, western provinces, 1st century A.D. Height 9.5 cm
Gift of Arthur A. Houghton, Jr. (57.1.4)

12.

Blown vase

Roman Empire, eastern
Mediterranean or Italy, 1st
century A.D. Height 11.7 cm
Some Roman blown ware had
dappled decoration, such as this
vase, which was covered with
chips of colored glass and then
blown, expanding the patches
of color. (59.1.88)

15.

Mosaic glass handled jar

Egypt or Italy, late 3rd–2nd
century B.C. Height 18.5 cm
(58.1.38)

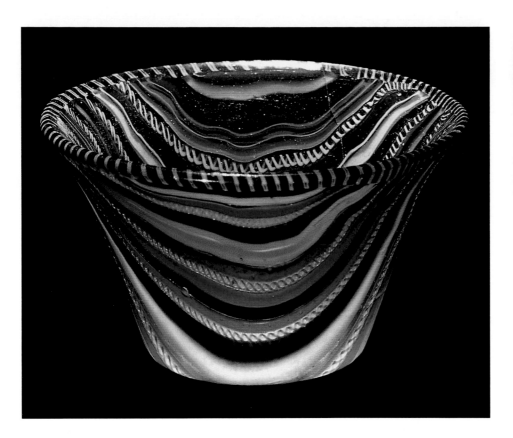

delight of the crowds. The fans would buy gladiator beakers as reminders of their favorite fighters.

Some Roman glassmakers inscribed their names on their glass. "Ennion made me" is one such inscription (pl. 13). Whether this was a testament to Ennion's pride in his workmanship, or simply an advertisement reminding the buyer from whom to buy his next cup, no one knows, but it may be one of the first sales slogans.

Romans particularly valued glass containers as shipping and storage vessels because they were transparent, reusable, and odorless, and did not impart a taste. Some were decorated with an image of Mercury, god of commerce, and they were packed in straw to survive long journeys by land and sea. Some were square for ease of packing.

At the same time that utilitarian glass was becoming commonplace, some of the most lavish glass ever made was being produced. The opulent covered box shown here (pl. 14) has gold foil laminated between strips of colorless glass. Some

17.

Cameo glass cup

Roman Empire, probably Italy, early 1st century A.D. Height 6.2 cm Many cameo glasses portrayed mystical scenes. Here, a woman makes an offering at a rural shrine, probably to ensure a safe childbirth. The cup was once in the collection of J. P. Morgan and is usually referred to as the "Morgan Cup." Gift of Arthur A. Houghton, Jr. (52.1.93)

elegant vessels were made of sinuous, fused rainbow-colored bands (pl. 16). "Gold-band" and mosaic glass toiletry containers may well have been among the most luxurious dressing table accessories ever made, and they emphasize the value placed on fine cosmetics and perfumes in Roman times.

Many Roman glassmakers sought to imitate rock crystal and other semiprecious materials. Layered stones such as those used for cameos—for example, onyx and agate—were emulated in glass (pl. 17) and carved in relief to reveal contrasting colors. To make glass using this technique, called cameo carving, the colored glass (often dark blue) was covered or "cased" with opaque white glass. It was essential that the two or more colored glasses be compatible in their rates of expansion and contraction; otherwise, fatal cracks would appear. Once cooled, the piece was handed over to the cutters. The true refinement of their art is exemplified by the fragment from a unique six-layer cameo glass cup (pl. 18), so finely cut that each layer was revealed, producing multicolored tonal and sculptural effects.

Techniques of painting and gilding on glass were also highly developed, the methods being not very different from those in use today. The basic techniques of painting were enameling and cold-painting. In the first technique (pl. 19), colored glass, ground into a fine powder, was mixed with oil until it had the consistency of paint. It was then applied to the glass vessel and heated until the enamel fused permanently to the surface. The Daphne Ewer (pl. 20), on the other hand, is a famous example of cold-painted, non-fired Roman glass.

Other Roman vessels were decorated by cutting, engraving, or abrading. In each case, the object was held against a rotating wheel fed with an abrasive paste. By varying this technique, the surface could be lightly or deeply cut, or abraded to produce a rough effect. The wheel-abraded bottle (pl. 21) shown on page 31 was probably a travel souvenir from a seaside resort in the Bay of Naples.

The rarest of all later Roman glasses are cage cups (pl. 22). Using wheels fed with an abrasive paste, the cutter removed

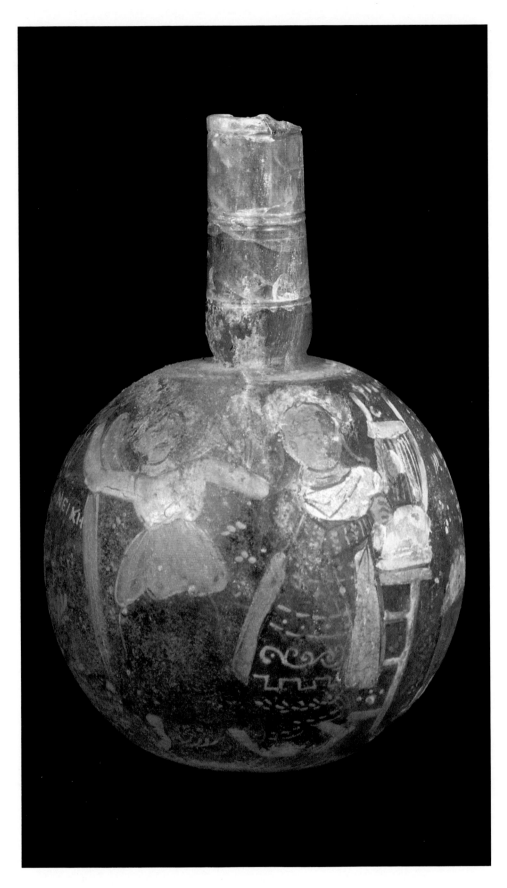

18.

Fragment of a six-layer cameo glass cup

Roman Empire, probably Italy, 1st century A.D.

Height 5.9 cm

The figure is Dionysus, the god of wine. (62.1.24)

19.

Enameled bottle

Roman Empire, eastern Mediterranean, late 3rd century A.D. *Height 14.6 cm, diameter 9.9 cm*

The mythological musical contest between Apollo and Marsyas is depicted on the surface of the bottle. Museum Endowment Fund Purchase (78.1.1)

23.

Snake-thread beaker

*Found in Worms. Roman
Empire, late 3rd–early 4th
century A.D. Height 20.4 cm
(82.1.1)*

20.

The Daphne Ewer

*Roman Empire, eastern
Mediterranean, 2nd–3rd
century A.D. Height 22.2 cm
The opaque white glass is
painted to depict the myth of
Daphne and Apollo. The god
Apollo, inflamed with desire,
pursued Daphne. In response to
her prayers for help, her father,
Peneus, transformed her into a
laurel just as Apollo was about
to reach her. (55.1.86)*

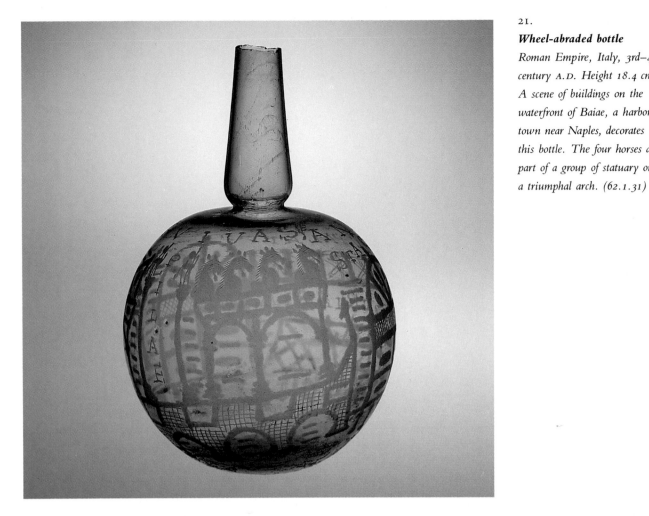

21.

Wheel-abraded bottle

*Roman Empire, Italy, 3rd–4th century A.D. Height 18.4 cm
A scene of buildings on the waterfront of Baiae, a harbor town near Naples, decorates this bottle. The four horses are part of a group of statuary on a triumphal arch. (62.1.31)*

22.

Cage cup

*Roman Empire, c. 300 A.D. Diameter 12.2 cm
Cage cups are the most complex glass objects made in ancient times. A single "blank" of colorless glass was cut and ground in the form of a bowl inside an openwork "cage." The metal attachments indicate that this bowl was used as a hanging lamp. (87.1.1)*

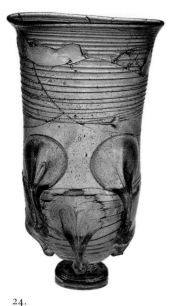

24.

Claw beaker

*Western Europe, 6th century
A.D. Height 17.7 cm
This characteristic Frankish
glass used hollow, clawlike or
trunklike projections as
decoration and to ensure a good
grip. (70.1.46)*

25.

Frankish cone beaker

*Western Europe, 5th–6th
century A.D. Height 23.5 cm
(66.1.247)*

most of the glass from a thick-walled "blank," leaving a cup- or
bowl-shaped vessel imprisoned in a fragile openwork "cage."

Glassmaking in the Roman Rhineland began in the first
century A.D. Some of the most beautiful glasses made there were
decorated with crimped strands of glass known as snake threads.
One of these glasses is the beaker from Worms (pl. 23). The
technique of snake-thread trailing originated in the eastern part
of the Roman Empire, but artisans in the Rhineland brought it
to its highest form.

The interiors of Roman villas were often ornamented with
inlaid glass and cast glass panels imitating jasper, porphyry, and
marble. According to Seneca, "A person finds himself poor and
base unless his vaulted ceiling is covered with glass." Inlays of
glass emulating precious stones may still be seen in the ruins of
Nero's "Golden House" in Rome. Glass was also employed for
lamps, hanging lights, and lanterns.

As the Roman Empire declined in the fifth century, its
armies withdrew from Germany. Local tribes, such as the
Franks, came to dominate the area. The Franks made simpler
forms of drinking vessels than the Romans. Some Frankish
glasses had clawlike projections (pl. 24). The shape of the cone
beaker (pl. 25) reflected the lusty Frankish drinking habits: a
glass was never set down on the table but was drained in one
gulp and taken from the drinker's hand to be refilled by host or
servant—therefore this vessel did not need a base or foot. During
this period, the Dark Ages in Europe (A.D. 476 to 1000),
glassmakers in general produced only modest vessels.

To the east of the Roman Empire, the Sasanians ruled Persia
(now Iran) from A.D. 226 to 651. They were a cultivated,
powerful people who enjoyed music, dancing, and hunting, and
their glassmakers developed a style of their own. This style was
distinguished by skillful carving in high relief (pl. 26) and the
use of applied trail decoration. The Sasanians traded their glass
throughout the Middle East, to Russia, and even to Japan, where
a number of examples have been preserved.

26.

Sasanian bowl with relief bosses

Probably Iran, 5th–7th century A.D. Diameter (top) 8.1 cm A great amount of time was required to cut away the surface between the bosses so that they would stand in such pronounced relief. (72.1.21)

27.

Octagonal pilgrim bottle

Eastern Mediterranean, 6th–7th century A.D. Height 10.8 cm Both Jewish and Christian pilgrim bottles, differing only in their religious symbols, were sold to pilgrims in Jerusalem. (50.1.34)

GLASS IN THE FAR EAST

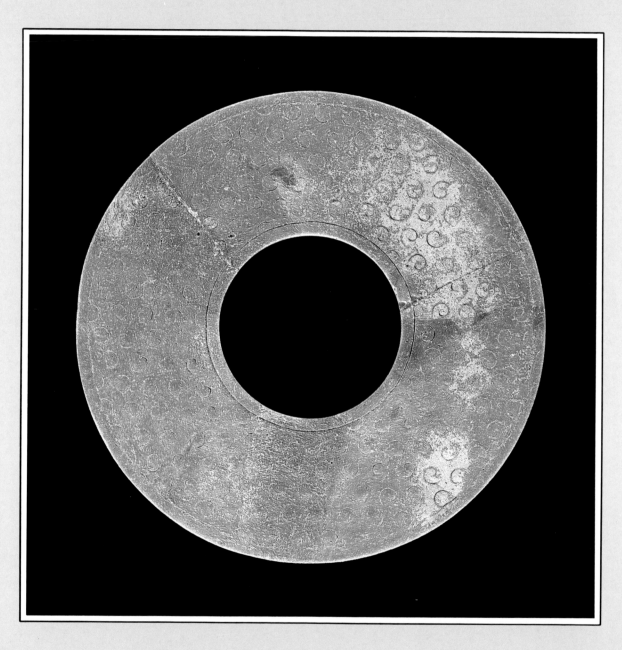

Glass beads with eyelike decorations, dating from the Warring States Period (475–221 B.C.), have been excavated in China. Their resemblance to Near Eastern eye beads suggests early trade links between East and West. During the Qin (221–206 B.C.) and Han (206 B.C.–A.D. 220) dynasties, contemporaneous with the Hellenistic and Roman periods in the West, the Chinese were making small, jadelike carved glass figures. *Pi* disks (pl. 28), which symbolized heaven, have also been found. Chemical analyses and other scientific studies have confirmed that all these glasses were made in China.

A poet of the Jin dynasty (A.D. 265–419) tells us that glass was imported to China, and he compares this glass to a spring day and its clearness to winter ice. Another early poet wrote of the difficult eastward journey of imported glass, recalling its lengthy trip across scorching deserts and over steep mountains. It is said that Chinese nobles and scholars of that time were so proud of their glassware that they invited guests for the express purpose of composing poems to celebrate their collections.

It is thought that in the fifth century, artisans from Persia went to China to make glass, and that at least one Chinese ruler sent a mission to Persia to bring back glass bowls and other treasures. However, evidence is vague until the end of the Ming dynasty (1368–1644), when Father Matteo Ricci recorded that he had astonished the Chinese court by showing glittering Venetian prisms. "At the present time," he wrote, "they make glass, but inferior enough to our own." Until then, glass as a medium does not seem to have held much interest in China except as an imitation of jade, coral, and other natural materials. The inherent

28.

Pi disk

China, probably Han dynasty, 206 B.C.–A.D. 220. Diameter 16.5 cm

The disk was a symbol of heaven. (51.6.548)

29.

Red cased vase

China, reign of Emperor
Qianlong, 1736–1795.
Height 49.2 cm
The vase has been wheel-cut
through the ruby layer to the
bubbly, colorless glass beneath.
The ruby layer was worked
three-dimensionally to represent
galloping horsemen brandishing
racquet-shaped objects; one
holds a pair of lances. The
neck depicts a temple with four
men on a veranda. All the
figures are shown in a craggy
landscape wreathed in clouds.
Gift of Benjamin D.
Bernstein (57.6.10)

30.

Five snuff bottles

China, c. 1800–1900. Height
(tallest) 8.9 cm
Gift of Marian Swayze Mayer
(82.6.19, .48, .40, .59, .16)

qualities of glass—its fluidity and transparency—had been largely overlooked.

By the eighteenth century, the preferred decoration in China was made by cutting, often cameo carving, of brilliantly colored glass vessels (pl. 29). Cut cased-glass snuff bottles (pl. 30) were in fashion, reflecting the highly ritualized use of snuff prevalent in China in the eighteenth and nineteenth centuries. (Snuff-taking is the inhalation of powdered tobacco.) Enameled imitations of fine eighteenth-century Chinese porcelain were also made by Chinese glassmakers. The pair of vases shown (pl. 31) was probably painted by artists at the imperial palace factory.

In Japan, early imports of Chinese glass stimulated the development of a glass industry paralleling that of China. This industry later produced styles characteristic of Japanese taste. Archeological finds of Western glasses, and some remains of local manufacture, have been uncovered in Korea, throughout Southeast Asia, and in India. Beads, bangles, and other small glass objects were made in India in pre-Roman times, and the production of blown utilitarian wares had been firmly established there by the Middle Ages.

31.
Enameled vases
China, reign of Emperor
Qianlong, 18th century.
Height 16.2 cm
The glass was intentionally
made to imitate porcelain.
(53.6.1)

ISLAMIC GLASS

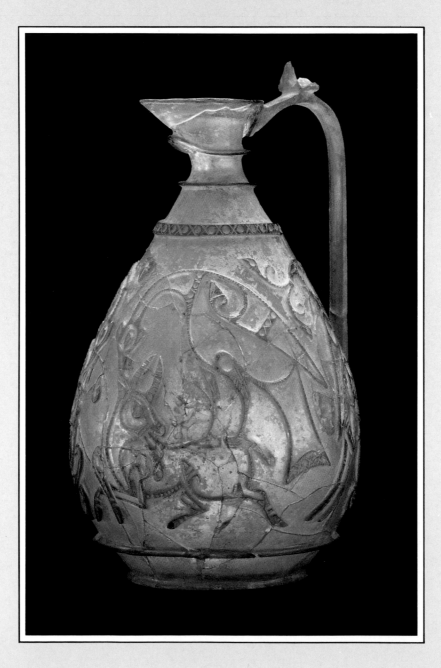

Duiring the Dark Ages in Europe, a new civilization arose in the birthplace of glass, the Middle East. Known as Islam, it developed between the seventh and ninth centuries and produced refined and elegant new styles of glassmaking.

The founder of Islam, the Prophet Muhammad, was born around A.D. 570 in the city of Mecca, in what is now Saudi Arabia. The word of Allah (Arabic for God) was revealed to Muhammad in a vision when he was forty. He became a preacher and in 622 established a community of his followers, called Muslims, in Medina, another Arabian city. Muhammad died in 632. Barely 100 years later, the Muslims had conquered a vast empire that absorbed the Sasanians in Persia and extended as far east as India and China; in the west, it included Spain, Portugal, and Sicily. Islamic belief has been so enduring that, with the exception of Spain, Portugal, and Sicily, all the former conquests are still partly Muslim.

By the eighth century, fabled Baghdad was the capital of Islam. Between 762 and 766, 100,000 workers built a new, circular Baghdad ringed by three walls of bricks. Baghdad's splendor-loving potentates encouraged an active cultural exchange—made possible by conquest and extensive trade—among Baghdad, Europe, and the Far East, further enhancing their opulent life-style.

The Muslims adopted something from every culture with which they came in contact. From the Chinese, who had reached such an advanced stage that their capital, Ch'ang An, was the largest city in the world, the Arabs learned papermaking. They translated Euclid's *Elements of Geometry* from the Greek. From

33.
The Corning Ewer
Islamic, probably Iran, 10th–11th century. Height 16 cm This exquisite object was blown of colorless glass covered with a thin overlay of green glass. The birds and animals left standing in relief show how much of the overlay was removed by the cutter. Clara S. Peck Endowment (85.1.1)

39

India, they adopted the numeral system which we use today. They also studied chemistry and medicine, established a postal system, and created literary works such as *The Thousand and One Nights*. By the thirteenth century, Islam was more advanced than Europe in medicine, mathematics, alchemy, and optics.

Though the Koran, the Muslim holy book, denounced luxury, Muslims gloried in sumptuous interiors and richly embellished bowls, bottles, and other vessels. These objects were often made of glass that had been blown in molds, relief-cut, or enameled. Perhaps this passion for lavish furnishings inside their palaces and holy places compensated for their harsh environment with its blistering desert and rugged steppe.

Glass that imitated rock crystal was treasured by Islamic princes. Some of this glass was thought to be as valuable as gold and silver, substances prohibited by religion. The relief-cutting on vessels was a difficult and costly process. It was achieved by outlining the design on the surface and then carefully cutting away the background to leave the design in relief, or raised. The rarest of all Islamic relief-cut glass was made with the cameo technique, having colored ornament against a colorless background. Relief-cutting is exemplified by the vessels illustrated here and on page 38.

32.

Relief-cut bowl

Islamic, probably Iran, 9th century. Diameter 14.1 cm Originally almost colorless, the bowl is now weathered and iridescent. It is carved with birds, ibex, and decorative motifs. Its original appearance may be imagined if one recalls that the poet Abu Mansur Mohammed compared a glass vessel to ice and water in clarity. (53.1.109)

Glass imitations of turquoise were so convincingly made that they were sometimes mistaken for the precious stone. The story is told that in 1472 a Persian ruler presented a turquoise bowl, already centuries old, to the Doge of Venice. On its base was inscribed "Khorasan," a province famous for turquoise mines. It is possible that neither the giver nor the recipient realized that the bowl was actually made of glass. (Today the bowl can be seen in the treasury of Saint Mark's Cathedral in Venice.)

Egypt, having now become part of the Muslim world, contributed importantly to the art of decorating glass by the refinement of a luster stain made with silver. A paste containing a silver salt was painted onto the surface of the glass object, which was then refired in a reducing (or smoky) atmosphere. The silver migrated into the glass and produced transparent amber or yellow colors. The same technique was used widely in stained glass of the Middle Ages, and is still used today.

Some later Islamic relief-cut vessels are known as Hedwig beakers (pl. 34), named after a European Christian saint, despite the fact that the glasses are probably Near Eastern in origin.

Detail of a sixteenth-century
Persian miniature showing a
bottle similar to the one shown
at right. (From the Houghton
Shah-nameh [Book of kings])

35.

Mold-blown bottle

Probably Iran, 11th–12th
century. Height 25.8 cm
A frieze of plants runs above a
Kufic inscription. The bottle
also has a band of applied
threads. Many Islamic vessels
had long, thin necks that
prevented the contents from
evaporating. (55.1.6)

36.

Enameled and gilded vase

Damascus, c. 1320–1330.
Height 30.2 cm
Fish, arabesques, lotus heads,
rosettes, and a repeated
inscription, "The Wise," form
the decor of this vase. The
lotus flowers are a clear sign of
Chinese influence because the
lotus was a typical Chinese
motif. (55.1.36)

Saint Hedwig is said to have used a glass in this style. She would
drink nothing but water from it, yet when her husband drank
from the glass, the contents had miraculously turned to wine. A
number of glasses associated with the saint, who died in 1243,
came to be treated as holy Christian relics. One, owned by Saint
Hedwig's sister, Saint Elizabeth, later probably belonged to
Martin Luther.

Images of living creatures were forbidden by the Islamic
religion; however, as with gold, the prohibition was not always
followed, especially when making objects for private use. If
Muslim glassmakers and other craftsmen represented human
beings or animals, they often did so in stylized form. Fish,
emblems of good luck, were a favorite decorative theme on
enameled glasses; they were thought to provide magical assurance
against poison. More often, however, Islamic glassmakers
decorated their wares with rhythmically repeated patterns of
plants (pl. 35), geometric designs, and quotations from the
Koran.

Of life in the great Islamic glass center of Damascus, a visitor in the fourteenth century wrote home:

Concerning the wealth of this city . . . which shows forth particularly in gold and silver, cloth of gold and silk, . . . incomparably fashioned with great art in the Saracenic manner, in glasses most pleasingly decorated which are commonly made in Damascus, we forbear to write, for they cannot be captured on paper nor set forth in words.

The glasses he was referring to were probably the enameled and gilded vases (pl. 36), perfume sprinklers, beakers, and bottles, which reached a height of artistry not equaled again until the Renaissance in Europe. One such enameled beaker is the subject of an English legend. The beaker, called the Luck of Edenhall, was probably brought to England by a Crusader, but the story says that it was left by fairies near a spring at Edenhall and that the luck of the residing family was dependent on its safekeeping. When one of the family took it, the fairy king warned, "When this cup shall break or fall / Farewell to the luck of Edenhall." The beaker is now one of the treasures of the Victoria and Albert Museum in London—intact, as is Edenhall.

One of the most lucrative branches of the Syrian glass industry supplied enameled lamps (pl. 37) to mosques, the Islamic places of worship. Mosque lamps housed a separate holder for a bowl of oil, on which floated a wick. These lamps not only lighted and decorated the mosques but were symbolic of the light of God as well.

The beauty of Islamic glass was marvelously conveyed by this Islamic writer some time in the eleventh or twelfth century:

He set before us whatever is sweet in the mouth or fair to the eye. He brought forth a vase, which was as though it had been congealed of air, or condensed of sunbeam motes, or molded of the light of the open plain, or peeled from the white pearl.

The manufacture of Islamic glass ended when the Mongol conqueror Tamerlane destroyed Damascus in 1401, carrying the glassmakers off to his capital of Samarkand.

EUROPEAN GLASS

During the Middle Ages in the Islamic Empire, glassmaking, other crafts, and learning had greatly advanced. Similar developments occurred in other cultures as well. During the Dark Ages in Europe, the Chinese were already printing books, the baroness Murasaki in Japan was writing *The Tales of Genji,* and in Persia Omar Khayyám was composing his timeless love poems.

However, for most of Europe's population in the Middle Ages, life was difficult, even precarious. People lived in small, isolated villages or on the land. Famine and plagues occurred frequently. Moreover, there was the threat of the Vikings, who captured people in central Europe to sell as slaves in the Middle East. (The Vikings were also discovering Iceland and Greenland and later, North America.) What learning and skills remained were preserved in the monasteries. European glassmaking was at a low ebb; only a few primitive vessels were being produced.

By the twelfth century, with the growing power of the Catholic church, the darkness in Europe began to lift. The development of Gothic architecture in northern Europe stimulated the production of brilliantly colored glass for cathedral windows at Chartres, Canterbury, and elsewhere.

Most stained glass windows illustrated Bible stories, and helped teach Christianity to people who could not read, which was most of the populace, including the lords and ladies. "Bright is the noble edifice that is pervaded by new light," said Abbot Suger, a churchman and statesman in twelfth-century France, speaking both literally and figuratively about the effect of these windows. To the abbot and others, the beautifully tinted light

39.
Cristallo goblet
*Venice, early 16th century.
Height 23.5 cm
Enameled and gilded cherubs
ride on garlands around the
glass. (53.3.38)*

47

streaming into the new cathedrals not only illuminated the tales of the Bible but also symbolized the truth of God.

In the south, where people were as unlettered as in the north, gloriously colored religious mosaics adorned churches in Greece, Italy, Sicily, and Byzantium. They were composed of colored glass cast as thin, flat cakes and cut into small pieces. By the fall of Byzantium in the fifteenth century, millions of these little pieces of glass must have been made to form rich, golden representations of episodes from the Old and New Testaments.

Although it has long been thought that the production of glass for church windows kept glassmaking alive during the Middle Ages, the best glassmakers of the period also created fine tableware (pl. 38). This utilitarian glass was made in both southern and northern Europe.

38.

Beaker and bottle

Probably northern Italy, 14th century. Beaker height 12.5 cm; bottle height 22.7 cm

The almost colorless glass was most likely made by carefully selecting and refining the raw materials. (87.3.33; 89.3.12, Gift of Alberta Stout)

Venice

The first important glass center in southern Europe was Venice. This city on the water was the major sea power and trade center at this time, a point dramatized by an annual rite performed by the doge, the ruler of the city. To the accompaniment of hymns, prayers, and guns the doge would toss a diamond ring into the Adriatic, thus "marrying" the powers of Venice to that of the water.

As the Islamic Empire declined, Venice became the crossroads of East-West trade and had a monopoly on commercial shipping to the East dating from the eleventh century. It was probably in the course of peaceful trade with the Middle East that Venetians received glass gifts and learned the art of glassmaking. In addition, Crusaders brought many fine specimens of Islamic glass to the Treasury of Venice's great cathedral.

So opulent was the shimmering, domed, and arcaded city of Venice that many treasures were bought and sold there: spices, scents, sable, gold, silver, jewels, ivory, ebony, silks, lace, damask, velvet—and glass. "All the gold in Christendom," according to one medieval chronicler, "passes through the hands of the Venetians." These wealthy, flamboyant men not only indulged themselves with exquisite glass, among other luxuries, but they marketed it to the world. By 1317, at the beginning of the Renaissance, Venetian trading ships laden with glass had already landed in Flanders, opening the whole of northern Europe to the influence of Venetian styles.

The Venetian glassmakers' guild was formed in the early 1200s. In 1291, the glass industry was forced by the authorities to move from the city to the nearby island of Murano—where it has remained to this day—so that danger of fire from the furnaces in the city itself would be eliminated and the glassmakers more effectively controlled. This was not such a hardship, since Murano was a summer resort where Venetian aristocrats had

Sixteenth-century view of the Piazzetta S. Marco, Venice, by G. A. Vavassore, after Jost Amman. (Courtesy The Metropolitan Museum of Art, New York)

View of Murano, 1559.
(Published by Matteo Pagan)

villas. The island was only an hour's row from Venice, and the lagoon between was studded on warm nights with gondolas going to and fro.

Though Venetian control over the glassmakers and their families was strict, these craftsmen were highly regarded. Many were given patrician standing, their daughters being permitted to marry noblemen. Control was crucial to Venetian trade because the glassmakers were privy to many jealously guarded secrets regarding the construction of furnaces, the formulas and proportions of ingredients, and the making and handling of tools. Glassmakers at that time relied on trial and error, using their eye, judgment, experience, and the knowledge handed down from glassmakers before them. Venetian glassmakers were not allowed to leave Murano; in fact, escape was a crime that carried the death penalty. There are stories of relentless assassins in pursuit of fleeing glassmakers—in one case, to the very gates of Prague. Yet many glassmakers somehow did succeed in leaving, and they set up manufactories in the Tyrol, Vienna, Flanders, Holland, France, and England. It was not until the seventeenth century that a book written specifically to instruct glassmakers was published by a Florentine, Antonio Neri. His book, *L'arte vetraria* (The art of glass), printed in 1612, made available to everyone secrets that had long been carefully guarded.

So important to Venice was the glassmaking craft that when Henry III of France visited Venice in 1574, it is said that his ship was greeted by glassblowers borne on a huge raft with a furnace in the shape of a mammoth sea monster spewing flames. (The king was then entertained at a vast banquet featuring a menu of 1,200 dishes.)

Venetians apparently made glass beads from the thirteenth century onward. The beads were used in rosaries and jewelry, and as barter for the African slave trade. Following the discovery of America, they became extremely popular with North American Indians. According to Christopher Columbus's log for October 12, 1492:

Soon after, a large crowd of natives congregated. . . . In order to win the friendship and affection of that people . . . I presented some of them with red caps and some strings of glass beads which they placed around their necks, and with other trifles of insignificant worth that delighted them and by which we have got a wonderful hold on their affections.

From the fifteenth to late seventeenth centuries, Venetian glass mirrors were considered the finest in the world. The glass, which had to be very even and clear to reflect properly, was backed with metal foil. Before this, mirrors had often been made of bronze, steel, or polished silver.

By the middle of the fifteenth century, and perhaps even earlier, Muranese glassmakers were making an almost colorless, highly esteemed glass called *cristallo* (plates 39 and 42), an allusion to rock crystal. They also produced a wide range of colored glass: dark blue, amethyst, red-brown, emerald green, and, later, milky white. In addition, they made various kinds of marbleized millefiori (meaning "a thousand flowers"), lace, and aventurine glass, the latter appearing to have been sprinkled with gold dust in imitation of the mineral aventurine. A sixteenth-century visitor to Murano, the Anglo-Welsh writer James Howell, had a fanciful notion: he thought the superiority of the island's glass was due to "the quality of the circumambient Air that hangs o'er the place." However that may be, it was the Venetians' skill that made their glass supreme, as the examples illustrated on pages 46, 52, 53, and 54, top attest. These glassmakers' elaborate vessels, often worked in complex, virtuoso shapes (plates 40 and 41), were sought as the height of grandeur by all who loved to make a splendid display of wealth.

Some gullible people believed that the best Venetian drinking glasses would shatter instantly should they come in contact with even a drop of poison—more a sign, perhaps, of the conspiratorial character of the times than of the nature of the material. In any event, Venetian glass was indeed very fragile; merchants complained constantly of excessive breakage in

40.

Dragon-stemmed goblet

_Venice, 17th century. Height
26.2 cm_

_The dragon motif, used in
Venetian and Venetian-style
glassware, may have come from
the story of Saint George and
the Dragon, or may have had
its source in the Far East,
where the dragon was sacred.
(51.3.118)_

41.

Covered goblet with white-striped decoration

Venice or northern Europe, late 16th or early 17th century. Height (with cover) 34.9 cm Twisted cables of white glass alternate with plain white stripes. The cables and stripes were embedded in a gather of clear glass, then pinched, twisted, and blown. (64.3.9)

42.

Wineglass

*Venice, mid-16th century.
Height 17.8 cm
This is actually composed of
three separate bubbles of glass.
Glasses such as this are seen
in late sixteenth-century
paintings. Such pure form
expresses the inherent qualities
of the glass and does not
depend on decoration or
complication. (61.3.135)*

43.

Covered cristallo beaker

*Venice or northern Europe,
c. 1530. Height (with cover)
29 cm
This beaker represents a purer,
less elaborate Venetian style
sometimes used for cristallo.
Such large cups served as
communal drinking vessels at
meetings of German guilds from
the Middle Ages to the
nineteenth century. This one is
inscribed with diamond-scratched
signatures of numerous members
of some such society. The
signatures date from 1574 to the
late eighteenth century. (50.3.1)*

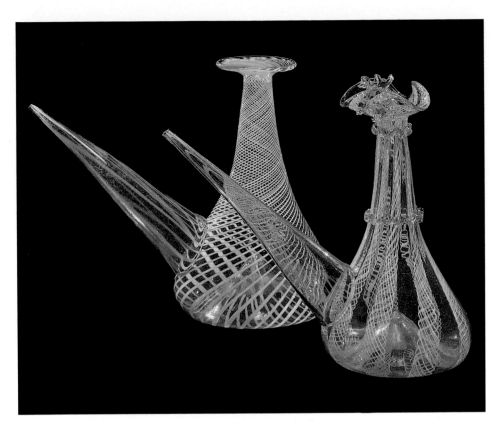

shipment. Vannoccio Biringuccio, a metallurgist, commented on this fragility in the sixteenth century:

Considering its brief and short life owing to its brittleness, it cannot and must not be given too much love, and it must be used and kept in mind as an example of the life of man and of the things of this world which, though beautiful, are transitory and frail.

Opaque enameled decoration on both colored glass and *cristallo* frequently portrayed classical themes. Other objects, such as the bowl pictured on page 56, were in the style of the painting of the time. Sometimes these scenes were shown on a field of gold that had been fused to the surface in the furnace.

Diamond-point engraving, which often consisted of simple and elegant floral motifs, was another popular means of glass decoration. It was also a natural development in Venice. Diamonds were just entering Europe for the first time, and because India was then the sole source, they probably all passed through the port of Venice.

With the progress of science during the Renaissance, glass
was found to be ideal for laboratory apparatus. It could be
fashioned into complicated forms, and it neither corroded nor
interfered with most chemical or pharmacological procedures.
Said one Jeremias Martius in 1584, "Man uses glass for many
things, but its service in medicine surpasses all others."

The optical properties of glass permitted improved eyeglasses
and the invention of microscopes and telescopes. (Without
Galileo's observations made possible by the latter, he might not
have conceived new theories about the cosmos. Unfortunately,
this also resulted in his imprisonment.)

While Venice was the dominant center of glass production in
southern Europe, glassmaking is known to have been practiced
since the twelfth century in the Italian village of Altare, situated
in the mountain pass where the Alps meet the Apennines. Little
is known about Altare glass, but it was probably similar in style

46.

Dragon-stemmed goblet
Probably the Netherlands, c.
1670–1685. Height 32.7 cm
Covered goblet
Stockholm, c. 1690. Height
46 cm
Two goblets, each with an
elaborate stem, show how the
Venetian influence developed in
northern Europe. (59.3.20,
65.3.56)

to Venetian glass. Many of the Altare glassmakers migrated, some of them settling in France. Unlike the Venetian glassmakers, who were forbidden to resettle, the glassmakers of Altare were actually encouraged by the authorities to go abroad and work.

Northern Europe

North of the Alps, anyone with pretensions to a refined life owned, used, and displayed expensive Venetian glass. The insatiable desire for this glass, its cost, and the difficulty of getting it caused many to dream of manufacturing it. Eventually, despite the ban on emigration, hundreds of Italian glassmakers were enticed to northern cities with promises of wealth and social prestige.

Although the influence of Venice (pl. 46) eventually dominated luxury glassmaking in Spain, France, Germany, the

47.

Waldglas *beaker*

Germany, 16th century.
Height 20.2 cm
The looped prunts on the side
are to help grasp the beaker.
Waldglas was made in the
forest glasshouses in Germany;
Wald is German for forest.
(53.3.2)

48.

Roemer

Germany or the Netherlands,
1600–1625. Height 27.8 cm
Sometimes these vessels were
enameled or engraved by
diamond point, but this design
depends on its own handsome
shape without benefit of
decoration other than typical
pointed prunts on its hollow
stem. (64.3.92)

Netherlands, England, and even Sweden in the sixteenth and seventeenth centuries, other kinds of glass were also being made in northern Europe, principally in the forest glasshouses.

Some forest glasshouses were large, long-lasting settlements complete with cottages for workers and a manor house for the owner. Others were small, sometimes short-lived enterprises near a monastery or the estate of a nobleman. In both cases, the systematic clearing of the forest for fuel helped to reduce the isolation of local villages. More importantly, at a time when famine was a constant threat, this effort cleared land for agricultural use. Consequently, the impact of forest glasshouses often transcended more than just glassmaking.

The forest glasshouses were run by families and guilds, which, like the Venetians, kept their secrets to themselves. To become a glassmaker was difficult because the guilds had uncompromising rules. "Nobody shall teach glassmaking," said one guild, "to anyone whose father has not known glassmaking. Nobody shall learn unless his father has promised and sworn and belongs to the guild and has made glass. The art may be practiced only by male children of legitimate marriages within specific glassmaking families." Boys entered the craft at the age of twelve, and they had to swear never to show "the said noble art, usage, and science" to anyone outside the guild.

Glassmaking was a rigorous, hazardous occupation. According to a book in 1713:

Certainly no one could endure for long the strain of such work as these men have to do, nor could it be kept up except by robust men in the prime of life. During the process of making glass vessels the men stand continually half-naked in freezing winter weather near very hot furnaces and keep their eyes fixed on the fire and molten glass . . . their eyes have to meet the full force of the fire . . . they shrivel because their nature and substance . . . is burnt up and destroyed by the excessive heat.

When undertaking the risky, tricky task of changing a cracked or worn-out melting pot while the furnace was roaring with flames, the forest glassmaker protected himself by dressing in garments and a mask or hood of the skins of wild animals. He was often black with soot from the fire, and his bizarre costume made him a terrifying sight—so terrifying, in fact, that some parents threatened to give their misbehaving children to this "monster."

The ingredients of northern forest glass were different from those of glass made in the south. The sand contained iron, which produced the typical green color of forest glass. Rather than import ingredients from the Mediterranean region, the northern forest glassmaker used wood ashes (potash), which were the natural by-product of his own wood-burning furnace. By carefully purifying the ashes and adding copper oxide, he deliberately nurtured the glossy green hue of the glass. Even after he learned to make colorless glass in the sixteenth century, he and his customers often preferred the typical green of his wares, enjoying the pleasant tint it gave the wine. Today, Rhine wine is traditionally served in green glasses.

The principal products of the northern forest glasshouses were window glass and large drinking vessels. Some of these beakers were of immense size, attesting to the notorious capacity of the users. The beakers had small knobs, called prunts, on the surface to allow a firm grip (pl. 47); the drinker's hands were apt to be greasy inasmuch as forks and napkins had not yet come into popular use (although affluent Venetians had eaten with forks since the eleventh century). In 1564, a German minister, referring to glassmaking in a sermon, spoke of these beakers: "Nowadays one applies buttons, prunts, and rings to glasses to make them sturdier. Thus, they can be held more easily in the hands of drunken and clumsy people."

A more refined drinking glass (pl. 48), called a *Roemer,* had a flared or rounded bowl; the prunts were confined to the hollow stem, where they still afforded a secure grip. *Roemers* are seen in many paintings of the time depicting both peasant life and high society.

Large cylindrical glasses, called *Humpen,* held several quarts of beer and were among the most popular enameled glassware.

The extraordinary size of so many German drinking vessels inspired one writer in 1688 to say: "You know the Germans are strange Drinkers. Every Draught must be a Health, and as soon as you have emptied your Glass, you must present it full to him whose Health you drank. You must never refuse the Glass which is presented, but drink it off to the last Drop. Do but reflect a little on these Customs, and see how it is impossible to leave off drinking. To drink in Germany is to drink eternally."
Le Buveur flamand (The Flemish drinker). Engraving by P. Chenu, after a painting by David Teniers, France, 1743.

49.

Enameled Humpen

*Bohemia, 1574. Height
26.4 cm
The double-headed eagle, or*
Reichsadler, *of the Holy
Roman Empire bears on its
breast a crucifix, and on its
wings the shields of the
electors, nobles, and others
owing allegiance to the
emperor. There were many*
Reichsadler Humpen, *and
they were so cherished that bad
fortune was thought to await
anyone who broke one. Gift of
Edwin J. Beinecke (60.3.4)*

Martin Luther called them "fools' glasses" and "obscenely large welcome cups," referring to the custom of draining one in a single gulp.

German and Bohemian glassmakers enameled drinking glasses with patriotic designs, biblical and mythological subjects, coats of arms, and scenes of daily life. Some depicted political themes such as the unity of the Holy Roman Empire (pl. 49) or the ending of the Thirty Years' War.

Many styles of engraved glassware produced in Bohemian factories and elsewhere became increasingly popular in the northern markets. Delicate diamond-point engraving (pl. 50) rivaled enameling as a desirable decoration. Diamond-point engraving required no prolonged training, the most important requirement being the ability to draw well. This made it possible for amateurs to pursue it as a hobby, often with calligraphy as their main interest. (Sixteenth-century Elizabethan poets sometimes engraved their verses on windowpanes in diamond-point calligraphy.) As glassmaking developed in the north and tastes changed, northern-made glass became more fashionable than Venetian glass (pl. 51).

The development in Bohemia and Brandenburg of a formula for a brilliant, colorless, easy-to-cut glass facilitated the perfection of wheel engraving. This formula used chalk as a principal ingredient, and its use spread quickly to other glass centers on the Continent. The hard-stone carvers of Prague, Munich, Nuremberg, and elsewhere turned from carving rock crystal and gemstones to cutting and engraving this new glass. They would press the glass against rapidly rotating wheels of copper or stone to incise designs and scenes. As in enameling, subject matter included coats of arms, portraits of princes, the ages of man, the seasons, mythology, and court life. The vessels were cut in sculptural relief or engraved in intaglio (cut into the surface), and they often reflected a richly wrought combination of both techniques (pl. 52) that has rarely been equaled since.

Bohemian glasshouses sent their salesmen throughout the world to seek new markets. Many of the vendors themselves

50.
Diamond-engraved dish
Probably France, mid-17th century. Diameter 48.8 cm, height 6.2 cm
The monogram may be that of Gaston, Duc d'Orléans, son of Henry IV of France. The eye of God shines down from above the monogram. The rim is intricately engraved with symbolic emblems, inscriptions, wreaths, and winged insects. Museum Endowment Fund Purchase (77.3.34)

51.
***The Maximilian* Pokal**
Nuremberg, 1690. Height 34.9 cm
This goblet was engraved and signed by Johann Wolfgang Schmidt, one of the greatest engravers who ever lived. It depicts Maximilian II Emanuel, elector of Bavaria. On the reverse side is a battle scene. Such goblets were elegant status symbols. Bequest of Jerome Strauss (79.3.158)

53.

Wheel-engraved plaque

Nuremberg, c. 1610–1620.
Height 15.5 cm, width
11.6 cm
Engraved by Hans Wessler,
a goldsmith said to have
introduced glass engraving to
Nuremberg. This plaque shows
Tomyris, queen of the
Messagetae, cutting off the
head of the dead Cyrus, king
of the Persians, who had
invaded her kingdom and killed
her son. (76.3.29)

were trained cutters and engravers who could decorate glassware on the spot according to the individual wishes of their customers.

England

Though glasses of a crude sort and fine colored window glass had probably been made in England since the thirteenth century, sophisticated glassmaking seems to have been initiated there, as in so many other European countries, by Venetian artisans. In 1571, Giacomo Verzelini and nine other Italian glassmakers came to London from Antwerp, where they had been living, to work in an English glasshouse. By 1574, Verzelini had received a patent from Queen Elizabeth to make glass in the Venetian manner. For about 100 years thereafter, the Venetian style dominated English glassmaking.

The Venetians were working in London during the Elizabethan Age, the time of William Shakespeare, Ben Johnson, John Donne, Christopher Marlowe, Sir Walter Raleigh, and Sir Francis Drake. England was in a period of expanding exploration, trade, and colonization; it was also faced with a severe shortage of wood needed for the ships engaged in these pursuits. By 1615, there was a prohibition against using wood for fuel. Glassmakers, switching to coal, had to overcome many new problems, such as how to prevent coal fumes from ruining the molten glass.

English glassmaking increased substantially with the mid-seventeenth century development in Britain of a black (actually dark green) bottle that protected its contents from light. This thick-walled bottle was also very durable, and few broke in shipment. With the advent of the black bottle, England became the foremost supplier of bottles to the Western world for more than a century. In *Robinson Crusoe* (1719), Daniel Defoe wrote that "great Numbers of Bottles . . . are now used sending the Waters of St. Vincent's Rock [an English spa] away, which are now carry'd, not only all over England only, but, we may say, all over the world."

An eighteenth-century English glasshouse. (From a 1747 engraving by C. Grignion.)

52.

Covered chalk-glass beaker
Potsdam, c. 1690–1700.
Height (with cover) 21.9 cm
The beaker is richly engraved both in relief and intaglio. Gift of Edwin J. Beinecke
(58.3.185)

54.

Ravenscroft Roemer

*England, 1676–1677. Height
18.8 cm*

This lead glass Roemer *bears
Ravenscroft's mark, a raven's-
head seal. The vessel is
decorated with mold-blown
ribbing, which is pinched to
form a mesh design on the
bowl. (50.2.2)*

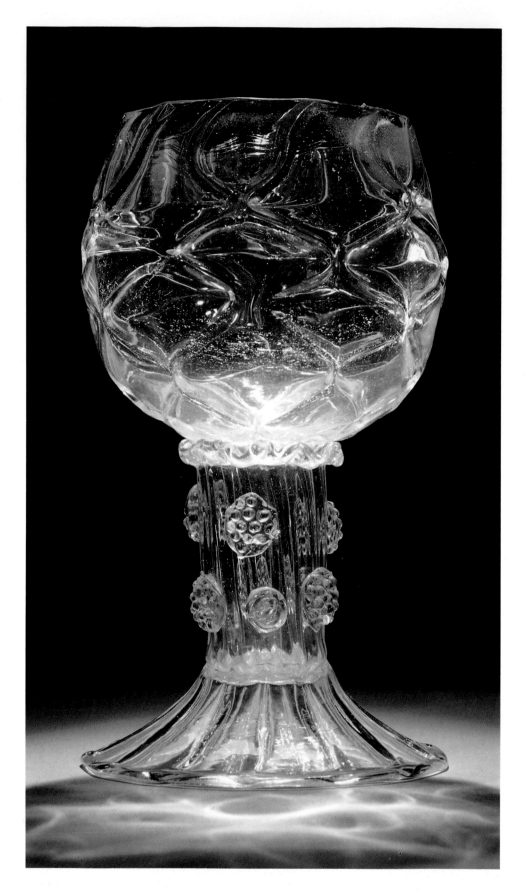

A clear, colorless glass less breakable than Venetian *cristallo* had long been sought in England. In 1676, working in London in great secrecy, an English glassmaker who had lived many years in Venice perfected a formula for lead glass. His name was George Ravenscroft, and his brilliant, heavy, resonant material is as highly regarded today as when he first developed it. Ravenscroft marked his new glasses with a raven's-head seal derived from his coat of arms. (One of his glasses is shown on the opposite page.)

Other English glassmakers soon took up making Ravenscroft's lead glass. It was essentially a new material, never before blown or worked by glassmakers, and quite different to work than Venetian *cristallo*. It remained in a workable condition longer; this property, combined with its weight, clarity, and capacity to capture light, led to a new goblet style: a simple, undecorated shape that relied on graceful form and fine proportions. A variety of new stem formations—using knops, balusters, teardrops, and air twists—provided a play of deep shade and brilliant light that had never before been seen in glass.

Engraved glasses carrying political messages were popular after the bloodless revolution that ended Roman Catholic rule in England and brought William III of Orange to the throne in 1689. Political sentiments were strong among both William's supporters (pl. 55) and his opponents, the Jacobites, who advocated the return of the Catholic King James or his sons. An inscription on one Jacobite glass reads:

> *God Bliss the Subjects all*
> *And Save both Great and Small*
> *In every Station*
> *That will bring home The King*
> *Who hath best Right to Reign*
> *It is the only Thing*
> *Can Save the Nation.*

Jacobites were liable to charges of treason for having such a glass.

Much lead glass was also used on the Continent, principally

55.
Williamite political glass
England, c. 1740–1750.
Height 19.6 cm
The inscription was both a hearty endorsement for King William and a no-nonsense critique of the Jacobite opposition: "To the glorious pious and immortal memory of the great and good King William who freed us from Pope and popery, knavery and slavery, brass money and wooden shoes and he who refuses this toast may be damned crammed and rammed down the great gun of Athlone." Bequest of Jerome Strauss (79.2.31)

56.

Diamond-stippled goblet

Frans Greenwood, Dordrecht, Holland, 1746. Height 25 cm Lead glass with a stipple-engraved portrait. (50.2.10)

57.

Enameled and gilded goblets

Newcastle-upon-Tyne, England, c. 1765–1770. Height 22.3 cm A brother and sister of the Beilby family, pre-eminent English enamelers, worked in Newcastle-upon-Tyne, where they practiced the technique of enameling clear crystal. These two signed goblets bear the arms, crest, and motto of the earls of Pembroke and Montgomery. (50.2.8)

in the Netherlands, where it was wheel- or diamond-point engraved. The most distinguished diamond-point engraver of his time was Frans Greenwood. He developed stippling, a method of composing a scene or portrait (pl. 56) by making dots (rather than drawing lines) with a diamond-pointed tool. Where the dots were close together, engraved areas appeared light and the untouched areas appeared dark. Diamond point had a delicate tonal appearance, while wheel engraving was usually more sculptural.

Glass cutting was introduced into England by German and Bohemian craftsmen, but a distinctly English style emerged by the middle of the eighteenth century. The surface was covered with an orderly geometric pattern of facets that brought out the high refractive index of the lead crystal, causing it to sparkle brilliantly. This style was used on drinking glasses, centerpieces,

candlesticks, and the newly developed prismatic chandeliers. Eighteenth-century rooms, even in richly appointed houses, were very dark and depended for illumination on candles, which were expensive and, in England, heavily taxed. Reportedly in 1772, Queen Charlotte's large dressing room, decorated with crimson damask, was lighted by just four candles. Only on festive occasions were homes brightly lit—as when in 1769 Lady Cowper wrote proudly that she had "an assembly in my great room, with about five dozen wax lights in the room." So, as cut lead-glass candelabra (pl. 58) and chandeliers became prevalent, their light-reflecting qualities multiplied the candlelight, enlivening many an elegant drawing room.

A heavy excise tax had been levied on English glass, but not on Irish glass. When Parliament lifted a thirty-five-year ban on exportation of Irish glass in 1780, the tax-free Irish glass industry began to turn out enormous quantities of glass for the large American market. Ireland became financially more advantageous than England for the glass industry, and much skilled English labor moved there. As a result, styles in English and Irish cut glass were similar, and even today it is difficult to tell them apart (pl. 59). Waterford, a name that has become synonymous with fine Irish glass, was the city in which one of the glasshouses

The glass showroom of Pellatt and Green. (Ackerman's Repository of Arts, No. 5, London, May 1809)

58.

Candelabrum

England or Ireland, c. 1785.

Height 90.5 cm

(50.2.23)

operated. An advertising circular from a glass store in Cork about 1790 gives an idea of the range of Waterford glass:

59.
Cut glass fruit bowl
*Ireland, c. 1790. Width
38.5 cm
(50.2.41)*

His shop is now completely stored
With choicest glass from Waterford—
Decanters, Rummers, Drams and Masons,
Flutes, Hob Nobs, Crofts and Finger Basons,
Proof bottles, Goblets, Cans and Wines,
Punch Juggs, Liqueurs and Gardevins;
Salts, Mustards, Salads, Butter Keelers,
And all that's sold by other dealers,
Engraved or cut in newest taste,
Or plain—whichever pleases best;
Lustres repaired or polished bright,
And broken glasses matched at sight;
Hall globes of every size and shape,
Or old ones hung and mounted cheap.

Waterford, Dublin, Belfast, and Cork were among the many cities that boasted a glassworks. These factories flourished until the mid-nineteenth century; in the mid-twentieth century some of them were revived.

Although some European glass had been exported to the Far East in the seventeenth century, it was the ascendancy of the English East India Company in the early eighteenth century that accounted for the great increase in English exports to India, both to English residents and to the native population. Among these exports was glass. For example, records show that shortly after 1721, five chests of glassware, together with a telescope and thirteen looking glasses, formed part of an outward consignment valued at £500, a considerable sum at that time. A 1737 advertisement mentions the export of more than 6,000 pieces of glass. The glass trade with India, combined with the American market for English and Irish glass, provided lively overseas commerce for the British.

AMERICAN GLASS

Glassmaking was America's first industry. When the Jamestown colony was established in 1607, the settlers brought glassblowers with them. However, the efforts to manufacture glass at Jamestown—and later attempts near Philadelphia and Boston—failed despite the abundance of fuel and good sand. Throughout the seventeenth and eighteenth centuries, the colonists imported most of their glass.

In 1739, more than a hundred years after the failure of the glasshouse at Jamestown, Caspar Wistar established a factory in southern New Jersey. Despite a British ban on manufacturing in the colonies, Wistar, a German, hired German glassmakers to produce window glass, bottles, and tableware (pl. 60). Benjamin Franklin used Wistar's scientific glassware in his electrical experiments. Wistar, the first commercially successful glass manufacturer in this country, began the German domination of the American glass industry that continued until the nineteenth century.

The second German to manufacture glass on a large scale in the New World, Henry W. Stiegel, operated a glasshouse between 1763 and 1774 in Manheim, Pennsylvania. Stiegel, too, employed foreign workmen, both from Germany and from England, and sometimes he lured glassmakers away from Wistar. The demand for all kinds of glass in the colonies was huge, and though most of the colonists' glassware came from England, Stiegel sold enough to prosper handsomely for several years (pl. 61). According to legend, he styled himself a baron and lived in a manner befitting nobility, even employing musicians to strike up a tune whenever he arrived home in his coach. He was an active churchman and deeded land to the Lutheran church in Manheim,

63.
Blown jug and sugar bowl with furnace-worked decoration
New York State, c. 1835–1850. Height (jug) 16.4 cm, (sugar bowl with cover) 27.2 cm
Aquamarine glass is typical of New York State glass, and these pieces were probably done on the worker's own time. They were made with hollow bulbs in the stems and below the hen-shaped finial of the sugar bowl cover. The bulbs enclose silver half dimes dated 1829 and 1835. Births, marriages, and other events were often commemorated by the insertion of coins with the appropriate dates. (55.4.157, 55.4.131)

60.

Wine bottle

Wistarburgh Glassworks, New Jersey, c. 1745–1755. Height 23.5 cm
This bottle was impressed with an "RW" seal. It was made for Caspar Wistar's son, Richard, at the Glassworks in southern New Jersey. Gift of Miss Elizabeth Wistar (86.4.196)

asking in return only the annual payment of one red rose — forever. This "rent" is still paid by the church the second week of every June to one of Stiegel's descendants.

However, Stiegel overextended himself financially and was bankrupt by 1774. Wistar's glasshouse closed in 1776, probably because of the disruption in business caused by the American Revolution. Only a few pieces survive that can be positively identified as having been made at these factories.

A third German, John Frederick Amelung, opened a large glass factory in Maryland in 1784, the year after the War of Independence ended. (This was also the year Benjamin Franklin used glass in a new way — to make bifocals.) Over the next ten years, Amelung invested more money in glassmaking than anyone in America before him. He produced large amounts of impressive table glass, much of it engraved (pl. 62). Yet he, too, failed, eleven years later. However, Amelung left us the best of early American glass, some of it signed and dated.

An ironic contemporary view of the situation indicates that Amelung and other eighteenth-century glassmakers failed to establish a lasting glass industry because they overestimated the market: "Most new works have been begun too large in this country. If we built a glasshouse, it was at the expense of Thousands and calculated to cover all that part of the country with glass which was not covered by houses." It was not until foreign competition was halted by the War of 1812 that glassmaking really flourished in the United States.

Despite many financial difficulties, problems stemming from the War of 1812, and competition with the English, American glass production increased during every decade of the nineteenth century. Most of the glass was still primarily for bottles and windows. Tableware produced in bottle and window glass factories was usually made by the individual worker for his family and friends, often on his own time and at the end of his shift. This glass was frequently decorated with superimposed bits of glass and threads in the German tradition, with variations according to the whim of the workman (pl. 63).

61.

As settlers moved west of the Alleghenies, they constituted a new market. However, because glass was difficult to ship overland, most western settlers did without it until the industry, too, moved westward. A traveler in the Western Reserve in the early nineteenth century commented:

The furniture for the table is scanty and inconvenient, articles of crockery are few and indifferent. For want of a glass from which to drink, if you are offered whiskey (which is the principal drink here) the bottle is presented to you or a bowl or a teacup containing the liquor.

Conjectural rendering of one of Amelung's glasshouses, drawn by Richard Stinely.

64.

**Amber sugar bowl with
mold-blown ribbing**

Probably Zanesville, Ohio,
c. 1815–1830. Diameter 13 cm
(55.4.70)

62.

**Wheel-engraved covered
tumbler**

New Bremen, Maryland.
Dated 1788. Height 30.1 cm
Inscribed, "Happy is he who
is blessed with virtuous
children. Carolina Lucia
Amelung. 1788," this was
made for John Frederick
Amelung's wife. It illustrates
the biblical story of the angel
leading the child Tobias on a
journey to cure his father's
blindness. (55.4.37)

Another traveler, Henry C. Knight, wrote in a letter, "They have no cider or common beverage for tabledrink; but, instead for the ladies water unqualified, and for the gentlemen, either whiskey, or apple or peach brandy."

Early in 1797, the first glasshouse on the frontier was started south of Pittsburgh by the financier Albert Gallatin, later cofounder of New York University and Secretary of the Treasury under Jefferson and Madison. Later that year, James O'Hara and Isaac Craig of Pittsburgh started a bottle manufactory (the first bourbon whiskey had just been distilled by a Baptist minister in the bluegrass country of Kentucky). In Pittsburgh, river transportation to the entire western frontier guaranteed a ready market. Nearby coal deposits provided ample fuel. By 1818, when President Monroe wanted American cut glass for the White House, Pittsburgh was the place from which to order it. From Pittsburgh, the industry spread down the Ohio River to western Virginia, Kentucky, and Ohio (plates 64 and 65).

Skilled glassmakers were frequently on the move, seeking either better wages or the free land available in the western territories. This created a labor shortage and stimulated a need for greater productivity. Obviously, one way to speed production was to blow glass into a mold, as the Romans had done, producing shape and surface pattern in one operation. It was an idea already in use in England. The earliest American molded glass imitated cut glass (pl. 66). A housewife's book, published in New York in 1815, suggests: "Those who wish for Trifle dishes, butter stands, &c. at a lower charge than cut glass may buy them in moulds, of which there is a great variety that looks extremely well if not placed near the more beautiful article."

Bottles and flasks for liquor were also mold-blown; after the War of 1812, they were often embellished with patterns, scenes, Masonic symbols, the American eagle (pl. 67), and portraits of celebrities. George Washington's face appears on more than sixty different types of flasks. When Jenny Lind, the "Swedish Nightingale," was brought to the United States by P. T. Barnum

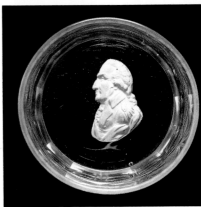

65.
Tumbler with cut decoration
Benjamin Bakewell's glasshouse, Pittsburgh, c. 1824. Height 8.5 cm
This tumbler has an enclosed molded portrait of President Washington in the base.
(55.4.57)

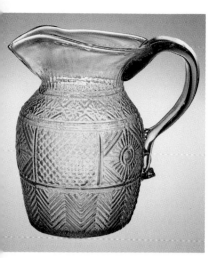

66.
**Blown pattern-molded
pitcher**
Boston & Sandwich Glass
Company, Sandwich,
Massachusetts, c. 1825–1840.
Height 16.8 cm
(55.4.204)

67.
**Mold-blown flask with
American eagle**
Probably Union Glass
Company, Philadelphia,
c. 1826–1844. Height 19 cm
(60.4.123)

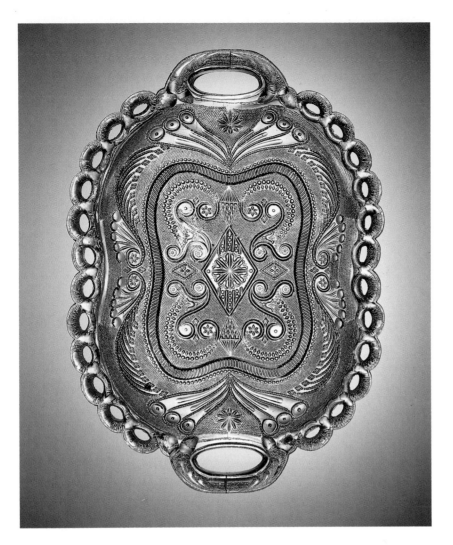

68.

Pressed plate with openwork rim

Probably Boston & Sandwich Glass Company, Sandwich, Massachusetts, c. 1830–1840. Length 30 cm (68.4.406)

69.

"Comet" pattern pressed glass

New England and Pittsburgh areas, c. 1850. Height (tallest) 34.8 cm Gift in memory of Amy Chace (68.4.12–23)

70.

**Kerosene lamp of
"Burmese" glass**

*Mount Washington Glass
Company, New Bedford,
Massachusetts, c. 1885–1900.
Height 48.5 cm
Gift in part of William E.
Hammond (79.4.91)*

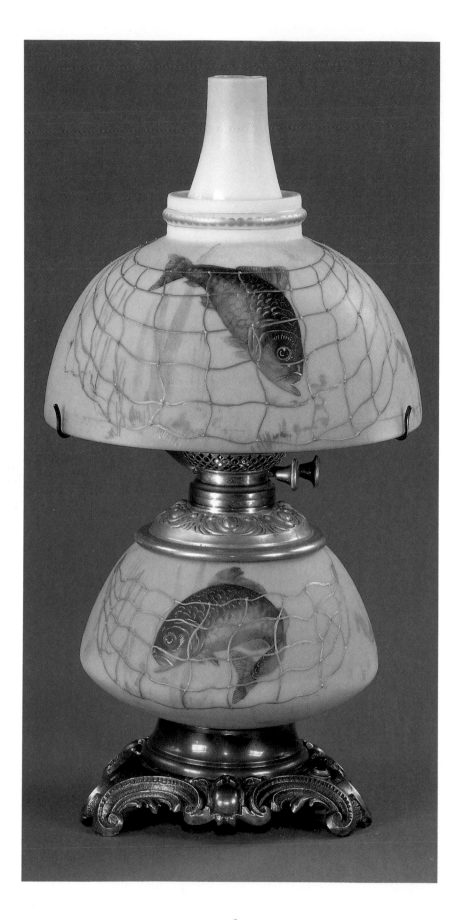

in 1850, several glasshouses were ready with bottles bearing her portrait.

While the use of molds speeded production, it was the development of the mechanical pressing machine in the 1820s that led to the mass production of American tableware. In fact, the greatest contribution of America to glassmaking, and the most important development since the Romans discovered glassblowing, was the sudden speed-up in the manufacturing process made possible by machine pressing.

At a pressing machine, two men with minimum experience could produce four times as much glass as a team of three or four trained glassblowers. A bowl came out of the press completely formed and decorated in a few seconds. However, because contact of the hot glass with the cold mold produced a network of wrinkles on some pieces, moldmakers turned from imitating cut glass to creating lacy patterns with a background of tiny dots (pl. 68); this way the wrinkles were "hidden" by the patterning. Technological innovations finally eliminated the wrinkles, and patterns became simpler in the 1840s (pl. 69).

71.

Cut glass plate
T. G. Hawkes & Co.,
Corning, New York, c. 1906.
Diameter 34 cm
This plate was made in the
"Russian" pattern. A large
service in this pattern was
ordered for the White House in
1891. Gift of T. G. Hawkes
& Co. (51.4.536)

A glassmaker's display at the Philadelphia Centennial Exhibition, 1876. At right is a pressing machine.

Pressing was used for candlesticks, vases, and table glass, and it facilitated the production of matched sets. It also made oil lamps cheaper and more widely available. At that time, whale oil was the most popular lamp fuel because it was abundant and gave what John Adams described as "the clearest and most beautiful flame of any substance that is known in nature." Whale oil lamps burned more brightly with glass chimneys, while the improved oil lamps invented by Ami Argand employed both a chimney and a glass shade to diffuse the light. At 10 candlepower, these lamps were considered too harsh by the standards of the day. Count Rumford, a scientist writing in 1811, said, "No decayed beauty ought ever to expose her face to the direct rays of an Argand lamp," and doctors warned of eyestrain for users. (It would require five Argand lamps to equal the light provided by one modern 60-watt bulb.)

A new lamp fuel, kerosene, began to replace whale oil in the mid-nineteenth century. Kerosene lamps *required* glass chimneys to burn properly, and so a whole new glass industry to make them was born. Despite the introduction of gas lamps, kerosene lamps (pl. 70) were the major home lighting device until Edison developed the electric bulb in 1879. The first light bulb blanks were blown for Edison by Corning Glass Works the following year, but electricity did not supersede kerosene lamps in the countryside until rural electrification began toward the end of the Great Depression.

By the mid-nineteenth century, American railroads and industry were growing, and the country was rapidly expanding westward. Economic prosperity increased steadily; Mark Twain called the period after the Civil War the "Gilded Age." With prosperity came a taste for complex decoration and ornate styles, greatly influenced by fashions from abroad. Some glass imitated silver, tortoiseshell, or Chinese porcelain. New shaded color effects were greatly admired, as were applied decoration and enameling. By the 1880s, American glass styles had exotic names such as Amberina, Burmese, and Peachblow. Said the *Crockery and Glass Journal* (1886), "Just at present, art glass is all the go."

Patterns in glass cutting were also becoming more and more elaborate (pl. 71); a decanter and wineglasses made for the Philadelphia Centennial Exhibition in 1876 were so profusely cut that not a half-inch of surface was left undecorated. (At the exhibition, there was also a glass fountain 17 feet high, ornamented with cut crystal prisms, lighted by 120 gas jets, and surmounted by a glass figure of Liberty.)

Glass containers (pl. 72) continued to be an important part of the American glass industry. In 1880, more than 25 percent of the glass made in the United States was for liquor flasks, patent medicine bottles, and the home preserving jars perfected by John Landis Mason in 1858. These were all produced by blowing into molds and hand-finishing the necks and lips. Patent medicines, promoted as cure-alls and often highly alcoholic, were a polite substitute for the liquor so frowned upon by the temperance movement. The bottles were usually distinctive and identified the contents: Turlington's Balsam of Life, Swain's Panacea, Perry Davis's Pain Killer, Lydia Pinkham's Vegetable Compound, and Hostetter's Celebrated Stomach Bitters. Just as in Roman times, glass was, and still is, the preferred container material for many substances—from food and beverages to scents, cosmetics, and panaceas.

In 1903, Michael Owens invented an automatic bottle blowing machine. For the first time, bottles could be made mechanically rather than by hand. The container industry was revolutionized. Later, other machines were perfected to make tableware, cookware, and fruit jars, putting more and more glass objects within the budget of most people. In 1926, the Wellsboro, Pennsylvania, plant of Corning Glass Works installed a ribbon machine, an automatic blowing device used primarily to manufacture light bulbs and, after 1939, Christmas tree ornaments. It could blow 2,000 bulbs a minute, nearly three million in a day.

72.
Flasks, jars, and bottles
c. 1840–1900. Height (tallest)
29.6 cm

NINETEENTH-CENTURY
EUROPEAN GLASS

D

Biedermeier Glass

uring the years between Napoleon's defeat at
Waterloo in 1815 and the revolutions of 1848 in France, Austria,
and elsewhere, the up-and-coming middle class in the Austro-
Hungarian Empire—especially in Vienna—enjoyed a prosperity
and domesticity whose ideal has been described as "happiness in
a quiet corner." It was the time of both Schubert and the
Viennese waltzes of Johann Strauss *père,* father of the composer of
The Blue Danube. Peace, comfort, and leisure were among the
most valued conditions of life, as was a well-ornamented home.
The crafts that enhanced domestic life—furniture, silver,
porcelain, glass—flourished.

Gottlieb (or "Papa") Biedermeier, from whom the period
takes its name, was not a real person but the fictitious author of
comic verse that appeared regularly in a nineteenth-century
German magazine. He was intended as the personification of the
Austrian bourgeoisie. *Bieder* in German means "plain" and
"inoffensive"; *Meier* is a common German surname. When the
term "Biedermeier" was first applied, it was used in a derogatory
way. However, by the end of the nineteenth century, the
Biedermeier style had come to be greatly admired for
craftsmanship and charm.

During the Biedermeier period, glassmaking was one of the
most important industries in Austria, especially in Bohemia. The
styles—despite the meaning of *bieder*—were hardly plain (plate
74).

By means of cutting, engraving, staining, and enameling
(plates 74 and 75), glassmakers lavishly decorated their wares
with city views, landscapes, allegories, flowers, animals, and
other themes reflecting the romantic, comfortable atmosphere of

74.
The Kulm Goblet
*Bohemia, c. 1835. Height
25.6 cm*
*This elaborately cut, engraved,
stained, and enameled goblet
exemplifies the essence of the
Biedermeier style. It is one of
four known goblets made to
commemorate the dedication of
a monument to the battle of
Kulm (1813) in the
Napoleonic Wars. (75.3.91)*

the time. Glass engravers and enamelers reached a peak of skill in portraiture (pl. 76). Much Biedermeier glass was created in various colors, some brilliant, others reminiscent of natural stones such as marble and porphyry.

Victorian Glass

An era that reveled in bustles, beaded reticules, fanciful furbelows, and in refinement, respectability, etiquette, and croquet, the Victorian Age was also the time when the British Empire was at its most prosperous and powerful, and the English middle class was coming into a position of dominance. Victorian glass reflected this prosperity and the accompanying love of elaboration, innovation, sentiment, and gentility. "The desire for decoration," said *The Decorator and Furnisher,* a periodical of the

73.
Cut glass table
Designed by Thomas de Thomon, The Imperial factory, St. Petersburg, Russia, c. 1808. Height 79 cm
Fine glass furniture has enjoyed an intermittent vogue from the mid-eighteenth century to the present day. This table, probably a present from Czar Alexander I to his mother or sister, was made of an octagon of blue glass above a spiral-cut amber glass column, the whole set upon a square amber glass base.
Museum Endowment Fund (74.3.129)

75.

Enameled beaker

Samuel Mohn, Dresden,
c. 1810. Height 10.2 cm
Employing translucent enamel,
Mohn painted minutely
detailed scenes, such as this
view of Meissen, maps of
celebrated battlefields, emblems
of friendship, and scenes of
daily life, and views of cities.
(51.3.198)

76.

Engraved portrait medallion

Franzensbad, Bohemia, dated
1834. Diameter 9.5 cm
Dominik Biemann was the
foremost engraver of his era.
This medallion bears his
signature, "D. Bimann."
(65.3.68)

time, "amounts to a perfect craze, and no one can tell when it is going to end."

The lifting of the excise tax on glass in 1845 and the 1851 Great Exhibition of the Works of Industry of All Nations, popularly known as the Crystal Palace Exhibition, in London further stimulated the glass industry. The Crystal Palace had its effect not only in Britain but all over the Western world. Organized under the leadership of Prince Albert, consort to Queen Victoria, the first world's fair was held in a gigantic greenhouse-like building that covered almost 20 acres and used some 400 tons of sheet glass, almost a million square feet. Three hundred thousand panes were hand-blown at a single glasshouse and installed within six months, enclosing an area four times that of Saint Peter's in Rome. No building on a comparable scale had ever been built, let alone covered with such a prodigious amount of glass: the Crystal Palace marked a revolutionary moment in the use of glass in architecture. Fifteen thousand exhibitors from nearly ninety countries gathered to show industrial art as well as handicrafts. Six million people visited the fair, which became the focal point of Victorian taste. Among the luxuriant objects on display, glass was prominent; in fact, the centerpiece of the Crystal Palace was a complex glass fountain ("the gem of the transept") 27 feet high. The Crystal Palace Exhibition was the first of a great number of international fairs that occurred nearly every year in the second half of the nineteenth century.

Large matching table services became more common and were all the rage at this time. For example, the "Axel" pattern, manufactured in Sweden, offered eleven types of stemmed drinking glasses, a water beaker, beer tankard, various decanters, ewers, jugs, dishes, salad bowls with and without handles, cheese dishes, sugar bowls and creamers, saltcellars, butter dishes, honey jars, tea caddies, flower vases, finger bowls, candlesticks, and bonbon dishes. Made to match were face-powder boxes, toilet-water flacons, soap dishes, water basins and jugs, and toothbrush holders—all of them magnificently decorated with rows of glittering cut facets and fan-shaped edges. Many elegant houses

*The Crystal Palace
Exhibition.*

could boast accessories of the boudoir that matched those of the dinner table.

Styles as well as functional forms were proliferating at a dizzying rate. A catalogue from one Stourbridge firm showed, on one page alone, 56 different styles of decanters—and offered 606 styles altogether.

The revival of earlier styles, such as Gothic and Renaissance, and the adaptation of "foreign" fashions, such as Egyptian and Moorish, typified nineteenth-century taste. Glassmakers attempted to keep pace with the succession of "historical" styles by copying earlier objects or inventing compatible forms to fill out services of glassware. One German lampworker adapted Venetian Renaissance designs so successfully that his glass has only recently been identified as being made in the nineteenth century (pl. 77). Complicated centerpieces in colored glass were

77.

Covered dragon-stemmed goblet

Workshop of C. H. F. Müller, Hamburg, c. 1880. Height 35.6 cm

Long regarded as a sixteenth-century masterpiece because of its remarkable Venetian style, the goblet was exposed as a nineteenth-century fake in 1978. (51.3.115)

ornamented with contrasting threads and prunts. Especially in Stourbridge, so-called fancy glass came into vogue, featuring fluted edges, applied decoration, and a wide variety of color combinations.

When glass pressing was introduced to England from America, the fantasy parade continued. Opaque and colored glass ornaments assumed countless eccentric shapes: boats, shoes, swans, setting hens, wheelbarrows, and baskets. Many pieces imitated cut glass.

The larger the Victorian piece, the better; centerpieces and glass lighting fixtures reached monumental proportions. In fact, such was the Victorian demand for grandeur in glass that, in 1895, the maharajah of Gwalior commissioned a pair of chandeliers that he desired to be greater than any in all of Buckingham Palace. When he was advised that such a weight could not be suspended in his palace, he hoisted three elephants to stand on the roof to prove that it would hold.

Bohemian wheel engravers, tempted by the prosperity of Victorian England, emigrated to Stourbridge, where they made relief and intaglio pieces of great brilliance, often on the newly fashionable Oriental themes. Perhaps the greatest of these Bohemians was William Fritsche, who eventually came to employ watery motifs particularly suited to his polished engraving style. A Fritsche ewer (pl. 78) was explained with thoroughly Victorian sentiment:

The whole ewer may be said to represent the progress of a river from its birth in a rocky hillside until it loses itself at last in the blue infinity of the sea. The neck of the ewer represents the mountain birth-place of the stream. The rush and hurry of the rapid river are wonderfully expressed by the strong, clear, curving volutes of the body. The lowest part is formed of a great fluted shell symbolic of the bottom of the sea. In this swim and sport a circle of vigorous dolphins.

The first European revival of cameo-cut glass since Roman times was yet another glory of Stourbridge, spurred by the work of John Northwood, who started in glassmaking at the age of

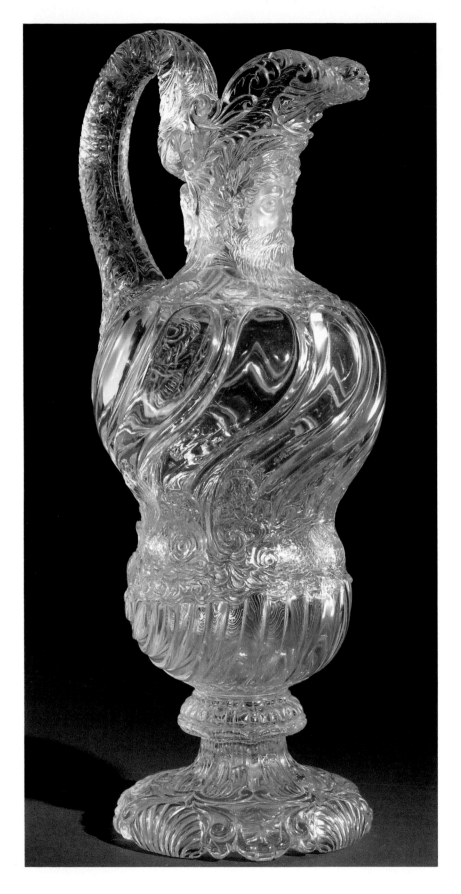

78.
Ewer with rock crystal
engraving
William Fritsche, Stourbridge,
England, 1886. Height
_38.5 cm_
Fritsche spent two and a half
years working on this piece.
_(54.2.16)_

79.
At Cupid's Shrine [?]
George Woodall, Stourbridge,
England, probably 1908.
Diameter 46 cm
This was carved from two
layers of glass, one plum in
color and one white. As the
white glass was worked thinner
and thinner, it took on a bluish
cast, although there is not any
blue glass actually in the piece.
The scene depicts Cupid and
Venus by a pool. (65.2.19)

twelve. Northwood later became famous for his adaptation in glass of the classic carvings from the Parthenon known as the Elgin marbles, and for his faithful glass copy of the famed Portland Vase, a Roman masterpiece of the first century B.C.

Cameo glass came in various colors, primarily blue or a plum color cased in white. A great variety of these works—vases, dishes, plaques, scent flasks—by Northwood, George Woodall (pl. 79), and others were produced with classic themes. "It may be said with truth," proclaimed *The Pottery Gazette* of January 1, 1908, "that no more noble ornament can be conceived in a room than a fine well-designed and artistically executed cameo vase; beautiful in form, in colour and detail, and at the same time having a gem-like quality which is truly precious."

Around the middle of the nineteenth century, glass paperweights (pl. 81) became popular. They developed at a time when writing paper was growing less expensive and letter writing was flourishing. Though they could be purchased at a modest price in stationery shops, paperweights soon came to embody all the most exquisite and bewitching technical effects of which glass is capable. Miniature, richly colored flowers, fruits, birds, reptiles, and commemorative portraits were encased in a heavy dome of clear glass, which magnified the motif. Cut facets were often applied to the dome, creating miniaturized, magnified, and multiplied images. Flowery and lacy effects were sometimes combined to produce delicate overall patterns. Small and fascinating, paperweights have come to be one of the most admired glass forms, sought by collectors all over the world.

80.

Table and boat

*Baccarat, France, 1889 and
1900. Height (together)
167 cm
These opulent objects are
typical of those produced for
world's fairs late in the
nineteenth century. An
identical table was owned by
Liberace, while another boat
was made for an Indian
maharajah. (79.3.155)*

81.

**Salamander or lizard
paperweight**

*France, Cristallerie de Pantin,
c. 1878. Diameter 11.5 cm
The animal's body is of cased
glass cut on the wheel to
simulate scales. The legs and
other details were added.
Salamanders were long revered
by glassmakers, for it was
believed that they could survive
fire without harm. Gift of the
Hon. and Mrs. Amory
Houghton (55.3.79)*

ONE HUNDRED YEARS
OF MODERN GLASS

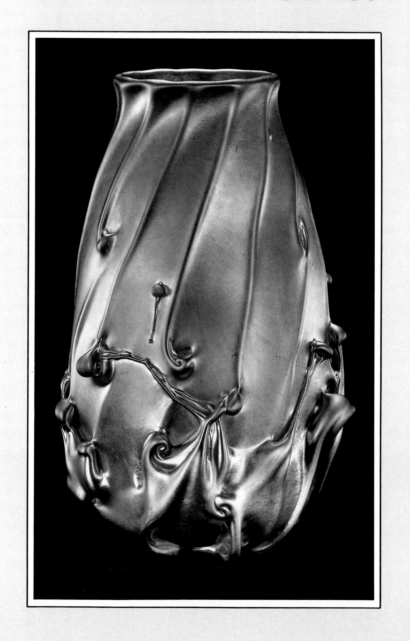

O f the many critical moments in the history of glass, five are of particular importance: first, the discovery of glass itself, more than 3,500 years ago; second, the invention, shortly before the time of Jesus, of glassblowing, allowing for glass to be available in large quantities; third, the development of lead crystal, with its greater weight and brilliance; fourth, the development in America of the mechanical press, resulting in lower production costs. At each juncture, glass was significantly improved.

The fifth turning point was of a different, nontechnical sort. It occurred a little more than 100 years ago, when designers and artists—who had not been glassmakers themselves—began to work in glass. Before then, glass design had usually been dictated by the skill, taste, and ingenuity of the artisan who actually made the glass or by the man who made the mold. By the 1870s, at least two artist-designers were working in glass, but it was not until the twentieth century that the designer and artist became important in many of the world's best glasshouses.

This involvement of artists and designers in glass manufacture led to the emergence of "art glass," what the French called *vases de délectation*. Designers created styles to be made by craftsmen in workshops or factories. Artists, including painters, designed glass objects too, and some also formed the objects at the furnace.

Among the first designer-artists to work in glass were Eugène Rousseau and Emile Gallé, both of whom became known for their glass at the Paris Exposition Universelle of 1878, one of the many international fairs that followed the 1851 Crystal Palace Exhibition.

89.
Gold Aurene vase
Frederick Carder, Steuben Glass, United States, c. 1910. Height 17.1 cm Tooled decoration and swirled ribbing add to the superb craftsmanship of this vase. Gift of Corning Incorporated (75.4.113)

Admiral Perry had opened Japan to trade with the West in 1854, and, by the time of the 1878 exhibition, Japanese art was much admired in Europe. Rousseau was greatly influenced by Japanese pottery and landscape paintings and prints. His work (pl. 82) was characterized by flamelike colored streaks and contrasting overlays. Sometimes he added crackle effects and metal particles. The objects were decorated with enamel, cutting, and engraving. Rousseau derived his forms not only from Oriental art but also from German *Humpen* and Italian Renaissance shapes. He made a significant contribution to glass design, although his career was short and his output small.

Emile Gallé is considered the mainspring of the Art Nouveau style in glass. During the 1880s and 1890s, Art Nouveau was a graceful style widely used in the fine and decorative arts: architecture, paintings, posters, book illustrations, furniture, wallpaper, fabric, embroidery, jewelry, and glass. It developed at a time when intellectuals and artists, rebelling against industrial production and historic revivals, were glorifying both the craftsman and the high standards of the medieval guilds. Richly ornamental and often asymmetrical, it employed long, sinuous lines, weaving tendrils, and flowing rhythms. Art Nouveau was a style particularly suited to the liquid, flowing qualities inherent in glass.

82.

Blown vase, with applied and engraved decoration
Eugène Rousseau, France, 1884. Height 9.2 cm
Gift of George D. Macbeth (62.3.112)

Like Rousseau, Gallé admired Japanese art—an admiration he expressed using themes from nature and a poetic mood in his glass work.

To Gallé, nature was the source of all beauty. He stated this belief in a sign on his workshop door that read, "Our roots lie in the soil of the woods, in the moss by the rim of the pool." Throughout his life, he was a practicing gardener and a learned writer on horticulture. He said that "each kind of plant possesses its ornamental style." He did not limit himself to elegant flowers, such as the orchids and lilies used as fashionable motifs at the time, but often used more homely plants, including the thistle and the pine (pl. 83). His natural themes were enlivened by stylized insects, especially dragonflies.

Gallé was also inspired by many of the Symbolist poets, and he often decorated his vessels with ornamental lettered quotations

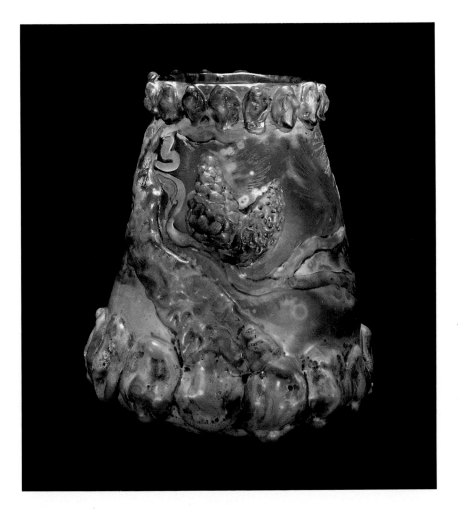

83.
Pines
Emile Gallé, France, 1903.
Height 17.8 cm
Blown amber glass and applied bits and trails of glass in the form of pine cones, pine cone scales, a branch, and needles make up this iridized, cut, and engraved work by one of the master glass artists of the twentieth century. Purchased with funds from the Clara Peck Endowment, The Museum Endowment Fund, and a special grant (88.3.31)

from Paul Verlaine, Charles Baudelaire, Stéphane Mallarmé, Victor Hugo, and Edgar Allan Poe, among others. The poetic quotations were always appropriate to the form and decoration of the vessels. Called *verreries parlantes,* these "talking glasses" were in the spirit of artists such as William Morris, Aubrey Beardsley, Dante Gabriel Rossetti, and—much earlier—William Blake, all of whom combined drawing and painting with poetry. Gallé made one such vase for presentation to Louis Pasteur, who originated the process known as pasteurization; it is inscribed with the following lines by Victor Hugo:

> *I move about in meditation,*
> *And at all moments a certain instinct obliges me*
> *To seek and find what lies behind the suffering of men.*

As Gallé's work grew in popularity, his establishment gradually developed into a large organization of craftsmen whom he carefully supervised. They carried out his designs in his personal, lyrical style. (After Gallé's death in 1904, the firm mass-produced numerous designs that did not receive the amount of care that had been customary in the making of his early works.) Gallé's glass was always signed, giving it the cachet of an art object and adding to its value for collectors. Other glassmakers soon began to sign their wares, too. Many other factories, such as Daum in France, Val-Saint-Lambert in Belgium, and Kosta in Sweden, produced glass in the Gallé style.

When Louis Comfort Tiffany, an American painter, visited Paris in 1889, he saw Gallé's fantastically colored glass at the Exposition Universelle and was deeply impressed. Tiffany was the son of the founder of the famous New York jewelry store, Tiffany and Co. He, too, brought a fine arts background to the design of functional objects—and he, too, was affected by the arts of Japan. His initial efforts in glass were in making stained glass windows (pl. 84), beginning in 1878. Like Gallé, he was a nature lover. He was also a leading interior decorator, with such eminent clients as the Union League Club in New York and Mark Twain, whose home in Hartford, Connecticut, he

decorated. Tiffany was invited to redecorate the White House when Chester Alan Arthur was president.

Tiffany's first collection of blown glass strongly expressed the Art Nouveau style. It was exhibited at the World's Columbian Exposition in Chicago in 1893, where it was an immediate success. The metallic iridescence, its chief characteristic, was inspired, he said, by the iridescence resulting from decay on excavated Roman glass. Tiffany's glass had a silky, delicate patina over luminous colors. The metallic luster was a film of metal produced by exposing the glass to chemical sprays. It was believed, erroneously, that $20 gold pieces were dissolved in acid and used as a source for the gold in the metallic film.

Tiffany's blown forms were often sensuous flowers on attenuated stems or other shapes that had rarely been used in glass containers before. These forms were decorated with lines and motifs that seemed to swell and narrow. One of his favorite patterns imitated that of a peacock feather. He also used many ancient techniques, such as millefiori inlay, intaglio, and cameo carving. Tiffany named his glass "Favrile"; according to a brochure, the word was derived from the Old English word *fabrile,* meaning "belonging to a craftsman or his craft." In Tiffany's catalogue for the 1900 Paris exhibition, he declared that "in none of the specimens of this glass is there any application of decoration by painting. Such designs as are found are in all cases produced by the combination of different colored glass during the operation of blowing the piece."

A French glassmaker, René Lalique, first became famous as a designer of Art Nouveau jewelry. Subsequently, he received a commission from the French perfumer Coty to produce special bottles for Coty's costly scents. He ultimately devoted himself completely to glass, which he called "an enchanted substance." The style most associated with his name is reflected in vases, bowls, and jars decorated in high relief produced by molding, sometimes accentuated by enamels, stains, or acid frosting (pl. 85). Among his most frequent decorative motifs were the human

86.
Acid-etched vase
Maurice Marinot, Bar-sur-
Seine, France, 1934. Height
17 cm
Gift of Mlle Florence Marinot
(65.3.48)

87.
"Negro Hut"
Designed by Edward Hald,
Orrefors, Sweden, 1918.
Height 26.1 cm
This piece was made in 1927.
(68.3.16)

figure, birds, fish, insects, and flowers, usually treated as elements in a formal pattern. Sometimes the pattern was purely abstract. Sharp and icy, Lalique's later style was the opposite of the flowing Tiffany glass and seemed at home in the Roaring Twenties, the age of the Charleston, the flapper, the first talking pictures, and sleek Art Deco interiors. Lalique's urbane style was related to the logical, sophisticated functionalist concept of beauty, which stated, among other ideas, that materials should be used "honestly," according to their nature, and that forms should be simple, and ornament geometric.

Maurice Marinot, who also believed in the functionalist definition of beauty, was originally a painter, one of the influential *Fauves* or "wild beasts" who also included Matisse, Rouault, Dufy, and Braque. In 1911, after visiting a glasshouse belonging to friends, Marinot became captivated by the qualities of glass as a medium. He tried enameling on glass shapes he had designed but not actually made; soon enough, however, he turned to making the vessels himself in a factory. He was the first artist we know of to choose glass as his medium and to work it himself. His massive vessels were deeply cut, heavily etched, and decorated with clouds of bubbles and subtle color effects. Unlike Gallé and Tiffany, he did not draw his inspiration so much from nature as from the qualities inherent in the material and from the process of working it (pl. 86).

At the furnace, Marinot worked by himself or with one helper. Working at the furnace was essential to him; it was there that his ideas developed. Echoing the experience of glassmakers past, he said:

To be a glassman is to blow the transparent stuff close to the blinding furnace, by the breath of your lips and the tools of your craft, to work in the roasting heat and the smoke, your eyes full of tears, your hands dirtied with coal dust and scorched. It is to produce an order of simple lines in the sensitive material by means of a rhythm which matches the life of the glass itself, so that in due course you may rediscover in its gleaming stillness that life of the human breath which will evoke living beauties.

Marinot gave up glassmaking in 1937 and returned to painting, but his work in glass had an impact on all the art glass that followed.

Another interpretation of functionalist esthetics, a style called Swedish Modern, came to prominence in household furnishings. This style is characterized by strong, clean lines and a natural use of materials. In glass, it emphasized the substance's "frozen liquid" character. It was first developed at the Orrefors Glassworks, then a small, little-known glasshouse in the forests of southern Sweden. In 1915 and 1917, Orrefors hired two painters, first Simon Gate and then Edward Hald, to design glass and to work directly with the craftsmen. This was the first time a glass company had hired artists. The style developed by Gate and Hald influenced glass design for many years. Hald was later to describe the role of the glass artist-designer thus: "An artist working in glass is primarily the director of a drama featuring the master and his colleagues plus a glowing lump of semi-molten glass."

Orrefors, with the help of Gate and other artists, produced a form of cased glass called *graal*. In *graal* glass, colored relief

88.

Tableware, blown cobalt blue glass
Designed by Josef Hoffmann, Wiener Werkstätte, Vienna, c. 1916. Height (tallest) 32.8 cm (74.3.24)

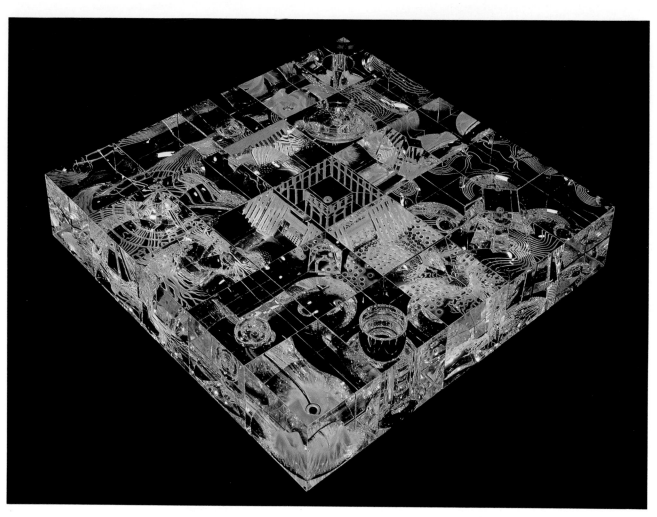

90.

Innerland

Designed by Eric Hilton, Steuben Glass, United States, 1976–1980. Height 9.9 cm, width 49.3 cm

Hilton, a Scotsman, designed this imaginary landscape, which reflects his fascination with Celtic mythology and designs. The 38 sandblasted, cut, and engraved parts were made over a period of four years. Anonymous gift (86.4.180)

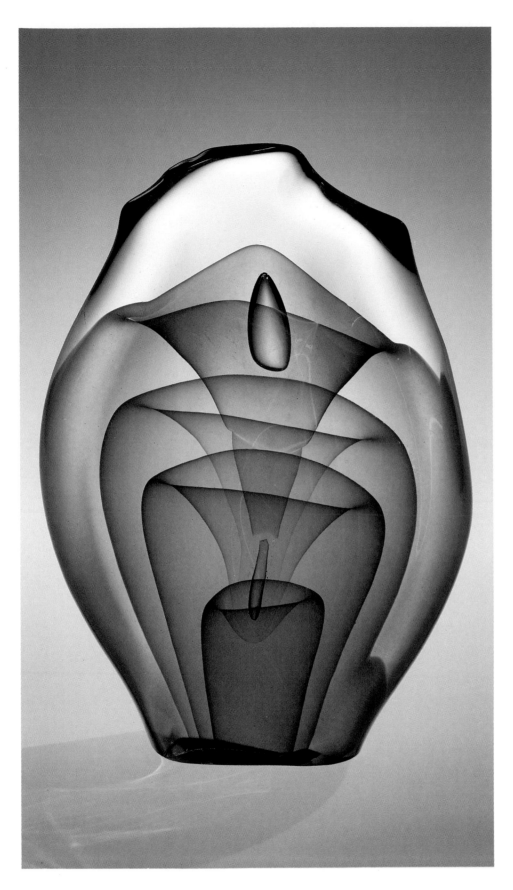

91.

Emergence Four-Stage

Dominick Labino, United States, 1975. Height 22.4 cm This solid mass of glass was sculpted while hot. The interior is decorated with air traps and veiled pink layers made by using gold. Purchased with the aid of funds from the National Endowment for the Arts (76.4.21)

92.

Foursquare

Harvey K. Littleton, United States, 1975. Height 13.4 cm, width (at widest point) 24.6 cm

The four semicircular sections consist of blown and cut nested forms. (75.4.54)

decorations like those used by Gallé were covered with clear crystal, thus acquiring a smooth outer surface over what then became an inner relief. The glass was then blown, expanding the trapped decoration. Under the direction of Gate and Hald (pl. 87), Orrefors also produced luxurious engraved works, some deeply carved and others with shallow engraving. Eventually, the Swedish style and the hiring of artists as designers were adopted by other Scandinavian factories such as Kosta and Boda.

At about the same time in Vienna, designers led by the architect and designer Josef Hoffmann were producing simple, functional wares based on geometric shapes, the forerunners of much glass made today (pl. 88). Among the firms for which Hoffmann designed was J. & L. Lobmeyr, which made glass of a dignified classical style in Vienna for three generations. In 1918, Stefan Rath, a Lobmeyr nephew, founded a branch of the company that made glass engraved according to the designs of artists.

In 1903, a glassmaker named Frederick Carder founded Steuben Glass in Corning, New York. He had emigrated from Stourbridge, England, at the invitation of T. G. Hawkes & Co., an American firm noted for cut and engraved glass. Though Hawkes intended that Carder would produce only blanks for cutting and engraving, Carder immediately also began to make a variety of lustrous lead glass in many colors and styles, including Art Nouveau. In 1918, Corning Glass Works bought Steuben Glass from Carder, who continued to design for the company until about 1936 (pl. 89). When Arthur A. Houghton, Jr., great-grandson of the founder of Corning Glass Works, became Steuben's president in 1933, he brought together architects and artists, including John Gates and Sidney Waugh, as designers. Corning scientists had just developed a new optical glass for lenses; it was of such unusual brilliance, purity, and workability that Houghton decided to use this material exclusively, thus ending Steuben's production of colored glass. Almost immediately, the Steuben design team established a new, distinctive style in a material virtually free of flaws. Within a few

93.
Curtain Raiser—
Zwischenakt
Jochem Poensgen, Federal
Republic of Germany, 1980.
Height 143.6 cm, width
190.5 cm
"Antique" and opal flashed
glass was cut, enameled, and
leaded to create this imposing
piece. Artists in the Federal
Republic of Germany have led
an international revitalization
of stained glass during the past
two decades. (88.3.1)

years, Steuben glass was being exhibited at expositions, galleries, and major museums. The company has continued to use only clear, highly refractive lead crystal (pl. 90) and to employ and commission designers and artists to produce new designs— functional and ornamental, abstract and representational. Steuben glass has been presented as state gifts by every United States president since Harry S. Truman.

In Czechoslovakia, the great tradition of Bohemian engraving continued until World War II. After that war, the Bohemian technical tradition burgeoned into a sculptural style, still evolving today (see page 110), that has had an important effect on contemporary glass around the world. The sculptures are usually one-of-a-kind works made in private studios or under the supervision of glass artists during factory time set aside by

94.

Littleton the Teacher

Erwin Eisch, Federal Republic
of Germany, 1976. Height
50.3 cm

A portrait head of Harvey
Littleton, one of the founders
of the studio movement in
glass, by Eisch, a leading
European glass artist. The
head is one of a series, made
by blowing a bubble of glass
into a mold and further
shaping it after removing it
from the mold. The surface is
enameled, and the interior is
silvered. (76.3.32C)

the Czech government. Special programs in Czech schools train
students in glass design and production. Among the important
contemporary Czech glass artists are František Vízner, Břetislav
Novák, Jr., René Roubíček, Stanislav Libenský, Jaroslavá
Brychtová, Pavel Hlava, and the engraver Jirí Harcuba.

In Venice, many well-known designers, including Tapio
Wirkkala of Finland and the American glass artist and teacher
Dale Chihuly, have worked at the firm of Venini.

Artists, especially those in Europe, have a long tradition of
working with glass, using such techniques as cutting, engraving,
and enameling. However, until the late 1960s, the vast majority
of blown art glass was still made in factories. In 1962, the artist
Harvey Littleton (pl. 92) led two workshops at The Toledo
Museum of Art; there it was demonstrated that glass could be
efficiently melted in a small furnace suitable for a studio with
limited space, yet still hold enough glass for the needs of a single
glassblower. By using such furnaces in their studios and by
forming the glass themselves, artists became technically
independent of the factory. They had become free to experiment
with molten glass as an artistic medium. The idea of studio-
made glass was soon introduced into advanced art education
programs, and it spread rapidly from the United States to
Europe, Japan, and Australia.

Today, not much more than 100 years after Rousseau and
Gallé began to make art glass, glass is recognized as one of the
materials of fine art, taking its place in the studio alongside paint
and the sculptor's clay and stone. Glassmaking is now taught in
art schools, craft schools, and universities around the world.
Sculpture executed in glass is displayed in museums and galleries.
While some glass objects made in factories have always been
non-utilitarian works created for ritual, ornamental, or esthetic
purposes, today most works that are esthetically experimental or
sculptural come directly from the artist's studio. In the past two
decades, a number of factories have recognized this and they are
increasingly employing studio artists.

In tracing the flow of glassmaking through history, we have

95.
Progressive Series #5
*Diana Hobson, England,
1986. Height 15.7 cm*
Pâte de verre *casting with
beach sand inclusions. A paste
of ground glass was brushed
into a mold and then fired in a
kiln to produce this extremely
thin-walled sculptural vessel.*
(86.2.7)

96.
**Pajaritos en la Cabeza
and Cabellos de Angel**
*Mary Ann Toots Zynsky
(American artist working in
Amsterdam), the Netherlands,
the third Rakow Commission
of The Corning Museum of
Glass, 1988. Height 16.6 cm
and 16.4 cm*
*Both are from the "Tierra del
Fuego" series, employing
pulled and fused threads of
opaque glass. (88.3.45)*

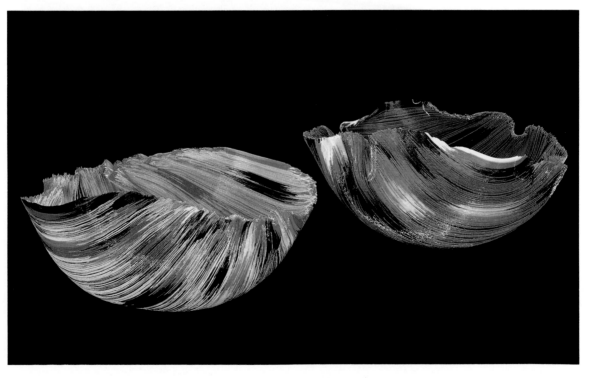

seen glass begin in ancient times as a wondrous transformation: ordinary sand turned into a precious substance. This substance was regarded with awe as a magical manifestation, and glassmaking's secrets were jealously guarded. In modern times, glass has retained its traditional fascination—its magical ability to capture and reflect light and its solid transparency, of being and not being at the same time. In *Remembrance of Things Past,* the French writer Marcel Proust said that glass is "real without being actual, ideal without being abstract."

Now, toward the end of the twentieth century, more than three millennia after its discovery, glass seems to have only begun revealing its magic and its marvels. New forms of this versatile material are enabling man to journey to the frontiers of science, not only in the laboratory and in industry, but also in space. In the 1990s, the American space shuttle—a vehicle containing critical parts composed of glass—is expected to put into orbit a telescope whose glass mirror will be capable of capturing light from stars 14 billion light years away. Since some scientists believe our universe was formed about 14 billion years ago, this glass mirror may provide a view of the creation of the first stars.

In the era when glass is taking us to the very edge of outer space, it has become a medium for exploring inner space as well—as an art medium with which the artist may transform a personal vision into a statement of universal meaning expressed in terms of transparency and light. In the coming decades, glass may well reveal not only more about our world, but also, as art must, about ourselves.

97.
Meteor, Flower, Dove
Stanislav Libenský and Jaroslava Brychtová, Czechoslovakia, 1979–1980. Dove height 222 cm, width 225.9 cm; overall maximum diameter 4 m 420 cm The symbols of this three-part installation, which was commissioned for the opening of the new Corning Museum of Glass building in 1980, can be translated literally: the meteor incorporates the logo of the Corning Glass Center, thus representing Corning as a glassmaking nucleus; the bird in flight stands for worldwide communication between glassmakers; and the flower suggests the eternal beauty of glass. (80.3.13)

BIBLIOGRAPHY

While any errors are the sole responsibility of the author, liberal use was made of the following admirable and authoritative books. The author heartily recommends these publications to the reader who wishes to learn more about the history of glass.

Arwas, Victor. *Glass: Art Nouveau to Art Deco.* 2d ed. New York: Harry N. Abrams, 1987.

Charleston, Robert J. *Masterpieces of Glass: A World History from The Corning Museum of Glass.* New York: Harry N. Abrams, 1980.

Corning Museum of Glass, The. *New Glass: A Worldwide Survey.* Corning, New York: the Museum, 1979.

————. *A Survey of Glassmaking from Ancient Egypt to the Present.* Chicago: University of Chicago Press, 1977. Text-fiche.

Frantz, Susanne K. *Contemporary Glass: A World Survey from The Corning Museum of Glass.* New York: Harry N. Abrams, 1989.

Klein, Dan, and Lloyd, Ward, eds. *The History of Glass.* Foreword by Robert Charleston. London: Orbis, 1984.

Newman, Harold. *An Illustrated Dictionary of Glass.* With an introductory survey of glassmaking by Robert J. Charleston. London: Thames and Hudson, 1977.

Polak, Ada. *Glass: Its Tradition and Its Makers.* New York: G. P. Putnam's Sons, 1975.

————. *Modern Glass.* New York: Thomas Yoseloff, 1962.

Spillman, Jane Shadel. *Glassmaking: America's First Industry.* Corning, New York: The Corning Museum of Glass, 1976.

Weiss, Gustav. *The Book of Glass.* Translated by Janet Seligman. New York: Praeger, 1971.

Whitehouse, David. *Glass of the Roman Empire.* Corning, New York: The Corning Museum of Glass, 1988.

An extensive reading list is available upon request from The Corning Museum of Glass.